CARDINAL RICHELIEU

CARDINAL RICHELIEU

Pat Glossop

CHELSEA HOUSE PUBLISHERS
NEW YORK
PHILADELPHIA

Chelsea House Publishers
EDITOR-IN-CHIEF: Nancy Toff
EXECUTIVE EDITOR: Remmel T. Nunn
MANAGING EDITOR: Karyn Gullen Browne
COPY CHIEF: Juliann Barbato
PICTURE EDITOR: Adrian G. Allen
ART DIRECTOR: Maria Epes
MANUFACTURING MANAGER: Gerald Levine

World Leaders—Past & Present
SENIOR EDITOR: John W. Selfridge

Staff for CARDINAL RICHELIEU
ASSOCIATE EDITOR: Terrance Dolan
COPY EDITOR: Richard Klin
DEPUTY COPY CHIEF: Mark Rifkin
EDITORIAL ASSISTANT: Nate Eaton
PICTURE RESEARCHER: Joan Beard
ASSISTANT ART DIRECTOR: Loraine Machlin
DESIGNER: David Murray
ASSISTANT DESIGNER: James Baker
PRODUCTION MANAGER: Joseph Romano
PRODUCTION COORDINATOR: Marie Claire Cebrián
COVER ILLUSTRATION: Philippe de Champaigne (courtesy of Jean-Loup Charmet)

First Printing

1 3 5 7 9 8 6 4 2

Library of Congress Cataloging-in-Publication Data

Glossop, Pat.
  Cardinal Richelieu / Pat Glossop.
  p.   cm.—(World leaders past & present)
  Includes bibliographical references.
  Summary: A biography of the able seventeenth-century statesman
who, for more than eighteen years, was the actual ruler of France
during the reign of Louis XIII.
  ISBN 1-55546-822-5
      0-7910-0704-9 (pbk.)
  1. Richelieu, Armand-Jean du Plessis, duc de, 1585–1642—
Juvenile literature. 2. Statesmen—France—Biography—Juvenile
literature. 3. Cardinals—France—Biography—Juvenile literature.
4. France—History—Louis XIII, 1610–43—Juvenile literature. [1.
Richelieu, Armand-Jean du Plessis, duc de, 1585–1642. 2. Statesmen.
3. Cardinals. 4. France—History—Louis XIII, 1610–43.] I. Title.
II. Series.
DC123.9.R5G56   1990
944′.032′092—dc20   89–49281
[B]   CIP
[92]   AC

Contents

John Adams
John Quincy Adams
Konrad Adenauer
Alexander the Great
Salvador Allende
Marc Antony
Corazon Aquino
Yasir Arafat
King Arthur
Hafez al-Assad
Kemal Atatürk
Attila
Clement Attlee
Augustus Caesar
Menachem Begin
David Ben-Gurion
Otto von Bismarck
Léon Blum
Simon Bolívar
Cesare Borgia
Willy Brandt
Leonid Brezhnev
Julius Caesar
John Calvin
Jimmy Carter
Fidel Castro
Catherine the Great
Charlemagne
Chiang Kai-Shek
Winston Churchill
Georges Clemenceau
Cleopatra
Constantine the Great
Hernán Cortés
Oliver Cromwell
Georges-Jacques
  Danton
Jefferson Davis
Moshe Dayan
Charles de Gaulle
Eamon De Valera
Eugene Debs
Deng Xiaoping
Benjamin Disraeli
Alexander Dubček
François & Jean-Claude
  Duvalier
Dwight Eisenhower
Eleanor of Aquitaine
Elizabeth I
Faisal
Ferdinand & Isabella
Francisco Franco
Benjamin Franklin

Frederick the Great
Indira Gandhi
Mohandas Gandhi
Giuseppe Garibaldi
Amin & Bashir Gemayel
Genghis Khan
William Gladstone
Mikhail Gorbachev
Ulysses S. Grant
Ernesto "Che" Guevara
Tenzin Gyatso
Alexander Hamilton
Dag Hammarskjöld
Henry VIII
Henry of Navarre
Paul von Hindenburg
Hirohito
Adolf Hitler
Ho Chi Minh
King Hussein
Ivan the Terrible
Andrew Jackson
James I
Wojciech Jaruzelski
Thomas Jefferson
Joan of Arc
Pope John XXIII
Pope John Paul II
Lyndon Johnson
Benito Juárez
John Kennedy
Robert Kennedy
Jomo Kenyatta
Ayatollah Khomeini
Nikita Khrushchev
Kim Il Sung
Martin Luther King, Jr.
Henry Kissinger
Kublai Khan
Lafayette
Robert E. Lee
Vladimir Lenin
Abraham Lincoln
David Lloyd George
Louis XIV
Martin Luther
Judas Maccabeus
James Madison
Nelson & Winnie
  Mandela
Mao Zedong
Ferdinand Marcos
George Marshall

Mary, Queen of Scots
Tomáš Masaryk
Golda Meir
Klemens von Metternich
James Monroe
Hosni Mubarak
Robert Mugabe
Benito Mussolini
Napoléon Bonaparte
Gamal Abdel Nasser
Jawaharlal Nehru
Nero
Nicholas II
Richard Nixon
Kwame Nkrumah
Daniel Ortega
Mohammed Reza Pahlavi
Thomas Paine
Charles Stewart
  Parnell
Pericles
Juan Perón
Peter the Great
Pol Pot
Muammar el-Qaddafi
Ronald Reagan
Cardinal Richelieu
Maximilien Robespierre
Eleanor Roosevelt
Franklin Roosevelt
Theodore Roosevelt
Anwar Sadat
Haile Selassie
Prince Sihanouk
Jan Smuts
Joseph Stalin
Sukarno
Sun Yat-sen
Tamerlane
Mother Teresa
Margaret Thatcher
Josip Broz Tito
Toussaint L'Ouverture
Leon Trotsky
Pierre Trudeau
Harry Truman
Queen Victoria
Lech Walesa
George Washington
Chaim Weizmann
Woodrow Wilson
Xerxes
Emiliano Zapata
Zhou Enlai

CHELSEA HOUSE PUBLISHERS

ON LEADERSHIP

Arthur M. Schlesinger, jr.

LEADERSHIP, it may be said, is really what makes the world go round. Love no doubt smooths the passage; but love is a private transaction between consenting adults. Leadership is a public transaction with history. The idea of leadership affirms the capacity of individuals to move, inspire, and mobilize masses of people so that they act together in pursuit of an end. Sometimes leadership serves good purposes, sometimes bad; but whether the end is benign or evil, great leaders are those men and women who leave their personal stamp on history.

Now, the very concept of leadership implies the proposition that individuals can make a difference. This proposition has never been universally accepted. From classical times to the present day, eminent thinkers have regarded individuals as no more than the agents and pawns of larger forces, whether the gods and goddesses of the ancient world or, in the modern era, race, class, nation, the dialectic, the will of the people, the spirit of the times, history itself. Against such forces, the individual dwindles into insignificance.

So contends the thesis of historical determinism. Tolstoy's great novel *War and Peace* offers a famous statement of the case. Why, Tolstoy asked, did millions of men in the Napoleonic Wars, denying their human feelings and their common sense, move back and forth across Europe slaughtering their fellows? "The war," Tolstoy answered, "was bound to happen simply because it was bound to happen." All prior history predetermined it. As for leaders, they, Tolstoy said, "are but the labels that serve to give a name to an end and, like labels, they have the least possible connection with the event." The greater the leader, "the more conspicuous the inevitability and the predestination of every act he commits." The leader, said Tolstoy, is "the slave of history."

Determinism takes many forms. Marxism is the determinism of class. Nazism the determinism of race. But the idea of men and women as the slaves of history runs athwart the deepest human instincts. Rigid determinism abolishes the idea of human freedom—

the assumption of free choice that underlies every move we make, every word we speak, every thought we think. It abolishes the idea of human responsibility, since it is manifestly unfair to reward or punish people for actions that are by definition beyond their control. No one can live consistently by any deterministic creed. The Marxist states prove this themselves by their extreme susceptibility to the cult of leadership.

More than that, history refutes the idea that individuals make no difference. In December 1931 a British politician crossing Park Avenue in New York City between 76th and 77th Streets around 10:30 P.M. looked in the wrong direction and was knocked down by an automobile—a moment, he later recalled, of a man aghast, a world aglare: "I do not understand why I was not broken like an eggshell or squashed like a gooseberry." Fourteen months later an American politician, sitting in an open car in Miami, Florida, was fired on by an assassin; the man beside him was hit. Those who believe that individuals make no difference to history might well ponder whether the next two decades would have been the same had Mario Constasino's car killed Winston Churchill in 1931 and Giuseppe Zangara's bullet killed Franklin Roosevelt in 1933. Suppose, in addition, that Adolf Hitler had been killed in the street fighting during the Munich *Putsch* of 1923 and that Lenin had died of typhus during World War I. What would the 20th century be like now?

For better or for worse, individuals do make a difference. "The notion that a people can run itself and its affairs anonymously," wrote the philosopher William James, "is now well known to be the silliest of absurdities. Mankind does nothing save through initiatives on the part of inventors, great or small, and imitation by the rest of us—these are the sole factors in human progress. Individuals of genius show the way, and set the patterns, which common people then adopt and follow."

Leadership, James suggests, means leadership in thought as well as in action. In the long run, leaders in thought may well make the greater difference to the world. But, as Woodrow Wilson once said, "Those only are leaders of men, in the general eye, who lead in action. . . . It is at their hands that new thought gets its translation into the crude language of deeds." Leaders in thought often invent in solitude and obscurity, leaving to later generations the tasks of imitation. Leaders in action—the leaders portrayed in this series—have to be effective in their own time.

And they cannot be effective by themselves. They must act in response to the rhythms of their age. Their genius must be adapted, in a phrase of William James's, "to the receptivities of the moment." Leaders are useless without followers. "There goes the mob," said the French politician hearing a clamor in the streets. "I am their leader. I must follow them." Great leaders turn the inchoate emotions of the mob to purposes of their own. They seize on the opportunities of their time, the hopes, fears, frustrations, crises, potentialities. They succeed when events have prepared the way for them, when the community is awaiting to be aroused, when they can provide the clarifying and organizing ideas. Leadership ignites the circuit between the individual and the mass and thereby alters history.

It may alter history for better or for worse. Leaders have been responsible for the most extravagant follies and most monstrous crimes that have beset suffering humanity. They have also been vital in such gains as humanity has made in individual freedom, religious and racial tolerance, social justice, and respect for human rights.

There is no sure way to tell in advance who is going to lead for good and who for evil. But a glance at the gallery of men and women in *World Leaders—Past and Present* suggests some useful tests.

One test is this: Do leaders lead by force or by persuasion? By command or by consent? Through most of history leadership was exercised by the divine right of authority. The duty of followers was to defer and to obey. "Theirs not to reason why / Theirs but to do and die." On occasion, as with the so-called enlightened despots of the 18th century in Europe, absolutist leadership was animated by humane purposes. More often, absolutism nourished the passion for domination, land, gold, and conquest and resulted in tyranny.

The great revolution of modern times has been the revolution of equality. The idea that all people should be equal in their legal condition has undermined the old structure of authority, hierarchy, and deference. The revolution of equality has had two contrary effects on the nature of leadership. For equality, as Alexis de Tocqueville pointed out in his great study *Democracy in America*, might mean equality in servitude as well as equality in freedom.

"I know of only two methods of establishing equality in the political world," Tocqueville wrote. "Rights must be given to every citizen, or none at all to anyone . . . save one, who is the master of all." There was no middle ground "between the sovereignty of all and the absolute power of one man." In his astonishing prediction of 20th-century totalitarian dictatorship, Tocqueville explained how the revolution of equality could lead to the *"Führerprinzip"* and more terrible absolutism than the world had ever known.

But when rights are given to every citizen and the sovereignty of all is established, the problem of leadership takes a new form, becomes more exacting than ever before. It is easy to issue commands and enforce them by the rope and the stake, the concentration camp and the *gulag.* It is much harder to use argument and achievement to overcome opposition and win consent. The Founding Fathers of the United States understood the difficulty. They believed that history had given them the opportunity to decide, as Alexander Hamilton wrote in the first Federalist Paper, whether men are indeed capable of basing government on "reflection and choice, or whether they are forever destined to depend . . . on accident and force."

Government by reflection and choice called for a new style of leadership and a new quality of followership. It required leaders to be responsive to popular concerns, and it required followers to be active and informed participants in the process. Democracy does not eliminate emotion from politics; sometimes it fosters demagoguery; but it is confident that, as the greatest of democratic leaders put it, you cannot fool all of the people all of the time. It measures leadership by results and retires those who overreach or falter or fail.

It is true that in the long run despots are measured by results too. But they can postpone the day of judgment, sometimes indefinitely, and in the meantime they can do infinite harm. It is also true that democracy is no guarantee of virtue and intelligence in government, for the voice of the people is not necessarily the voice of God. But democracy, by assuring the right of opposition, offers built-in resistance to the evils inherent in absolutism. As the theologian Reinhold Niebuhr summed it up, "Man's capacity for justice makes democracy possible, but man's inclination to injustice makes democracy necessary."

A second test for leadership is the end for which power is sought. When leaders have as their goal the supremacy of a master race or the promotion of totalitarian revolution or the acquisition and exploitation of colonies or the protection of greed and privilege or the preservation of personal power, it is likely that their leadership will do little to advance the cause of humanity. When their goal is the abolition of slavery, the liberation of women, the enlargement of opportunity for the poor and powerless, the extension of equal rights to racial minorities, the defense of the freedoms of expression and opposition, it is likely that their leadership will increase the sum of human liberty and welfare.

Leaders have done great harm to the world. They have also conferred great benefits. You will find both sorts in this series. Even "good" leaders must be regarded with a certain wariness. Leaders are not demigods; they put on their trousers one leg after another just like ordinary mortals. No leader is infallible, and every leader needs to be reminded of this at regular intervals. Irreverence irritates leaders but is their salvation. Unquestioning submission corrupts leaders and demeans followers. Making a cult of a leader is always a mistake. Fortunately hero worship generates its own antidote. "Every hero," said Emerson, "becomes a bore at last."

The signal benefit the great leaders confer is to embolden the rest of us to live according to our own best selves, to be active, insistent, and resolute in affirming our own sense of things. For great leaders attest to the reality of human freedom against the supposed inevitabilities of history. And they attest to the wisdom and power that may lie within the most unlikely of us, which is why Abraham Lincoln remains the supreme example of great leadership. A great leader, said Emerson, exhibits new possibilities to all humanity. "We feed on genius. . . . Great men exist that there may be greater men."

Great leaders, in short, justify themselves by emancipating and empowering their followers. So humanity struggles to master its destiny, remembering with Alexis de Tocqueville: "It is true that around every man a fatal circle is traced beyond which he cannot pass; but within the wide verge of that circle he is powerful and free; as it is with man, so with communities."

1

The Day of Dupes

Cardinal Richelieu believed that he was surrounded by enemies, and his fears were not unfounded. Eternal vigilance had become a way of life for him — it was the price he paid for being first minister of France and one of the most powerful men in 17th-century Europe. The cardinal was the eye at the center of a constant storm of intrigue and deceit. Plots and counterplots swirled, conspiracies were hatched; there were poisoned cups of wine on the dinner table and assassins with daggers waiting in the shadows. Abroad, the cardinal was threatened by the enemies of France and France's royal Bourbon line: the forces and allies of the extensive Austrian Hapsburg empire, which had dominated central Europe for centuries and which included Spain, the premier military power in Europe. At home, the cardinal was confronted with persecuted Huguenots, discontented French noblemen, devious Hapsburg partisans; in effect, all those who believed that the cardinal's influence over King Louis XIII of France had to end.

One must sleep like a lion— with open eyes.
—CARDINAL RICHELIEU

Born Armand Jean du Plessis de Richelieu in a Paris suburb in 1585, Cardinal Richelieu, the "Red Eminence" of France, was a man of burning ambition and cunning intelligence. Richelieu had one goal — to establish France as the dominant power in Europe.

Holy Roman Emperor Maximilian I of Austria (1459–1519) was one of the progenitors — along with Ferdinand II of Spain — of the European Hapsburg dynasty, the rivals of Richelieu and the Bourbon royal family of France.

In the autumn of 1630, the most formidable domestic adversary of Cardinal Richelieu's was neither a rebellious Huguenot nor a seditious nobleman — it was the king's mother, Marie de Médicis. It was indicative of the tangled and endlessly shifting state of political affairs in 17th-century Europe that the queen mother, who had once been the cardinal's staunchest and most powerful ally, now stood in the way of all Richelieu's hopes and ambitions for France. Of royal Italian lineage, she favored the Hapsburgs and the Spanish, and she was increasingly antagonistic toward the anti-Hapsburg cardinal.

Richelieu had long envisioned a France that might become the rival of the Hapsburgs and a major European power itself, beholden to no other nation or ruler. The cardinal, as the king's best friend and closest adviser since 1624, had carefully guided France and the French monarch toward this goal. But now the queen mother, feeling that she had created a monster in Richelieu, jealous of the cardinal's influence over her son, and hostile toward his political ambitions, was trying to convince Louis to dismiss the cardinal and to replace him with a cabinet — made up of Italians and Spaniards — that would answer only to her.

In Richelieu, the queen mother had found a most agile, and potentially deadly, opponent. At 38, the scarlet-robed cardinal was the most feared man in France. He was intellectually brilliant and politically ruthless, and there were few in France who had survived an attempt to dislodge him from his position at the right hand of the king. The cardinal was determined to elevate his country and the Bourbons to a position of greatness in European affairs, and he did not intend to let anyone stand in his way —not even the imperious queen mother herself.

Marie de Médicis had shrewdly begun her campaign against the cardinal at a time when her son the king was in a weakened and vulnerable condition. Louis had returned from a military venture in Italy exhausted and seriously ill. He was nursed back to health by his mother and his wife, Queen

Anne, at their palace in Lyons, and while he convalesced, safely out from under the eye of the usually omnipresent cardinal, the two women built their case against Richelieu. (Anne was also in the Hapsburg-Spanish camp, having been born a princess of Spain and betrothed to Louis as part of a treaty between Spain and France in 1615.)

The cardinal, in the meantime, was in Paris, attending to affairs of state in the absence of the king. He knew that the queen mother was in Lyons with her son, agitating against him, and throughout the

King Louis XIII of France was a weak and indecisive ruler, and his reign was plagued by dissension and intrigue within his own family. Cardinal Richelieu provided France with the vision and conviction that the king lacked.

summer and fall he was kept abreast of the situation by his spies (Richelieu operated a massive secret-police network). By November it had become apparent to the increasingly nervous Richelieu that the king's loyalty to him had been undermined. The situation was grave. The cardinal had made many enemies during his rise to power, and without the sanction of the king he would inevitably fall into the hands of one hostile faction or another. Under the influence of his mother, it was even conceivable that the king might have the cardinal imprisoned — or executed. This, Richelieu believed, would be a disaster not only for himself but for France as well.

In November, Louis returned to Paris with his court. Richelieu decided to force a confrontation, hoping that the king's dependence on him would outweigh loyalty to his mother. There were deep emotional as well as political bonds between the cardinal and the king, but an attempt to come between a mother and her son was still a dangerous gamble.

On the night of November 30, Richelieu followed the king to the queen mother's quarters at the Luxembourg palace, flitting through the dark streets of Paris in his long robes. Using a secret entrance to the queen mother's private chapel, which was connected to her quarters by a dark hallway, the cardinal made his way unseen to her bedroom, where he surprised the queen mother and her son, who were deep in conversation. "I wager that you are talking about me," Richelieu said. The queen mother, outraged by the bold intrusion, exploded, demanding that Richelieu get out. Instead, the cardinal threw himself at the feet of the king. For Louis, the choice was clear — his mother or the cardinal. To the dismay of Richelieu, the king ordered him to withdraw. Then, disgusted by the entire scene, Louis departed for his hunting lodge at Versailles to contemplate his decision.

The queen mother, and most court observers, believed she had triumphed over the cardinal. She began to gather a shadow cabinet about her at the Luxembourg, in preparation for her assumption of power. Richelieu also believed that Marie de Médicis had won the power struggle. When he was summoned to Versailles by the king, he considered fleeing but decided against it; if he could not dedicate his life to the service of France and the king, then his life was not worth living. He would go to his king and meet his fate.

It was not death at the hands of the executioner or imprisonment in some dank Bastille dungeon or exile that awaited Cardinal Richelieu at Versailles. Rather, it was the king's embrace, which told the cardinal that he would remain in power. He had surpassed even the queen mother in the affections of Louis. The queen mother and her supporters, fearing the wrath of the cardinal, quickly vacated the Luxembourg and went into exile. (Those who did not escape were imprisoned for life or beheaded.) The people of France, for their part, began to refer to November 30 as the Day of Dupes, for that was the day that the queen mother, her allies, and the French had been duped into thinking that Cardinal Richelieu could be brought to his knees.

Regi Armandus, the banner over the infant's cradle proclaimed; "Armand for the King." The streamer was intended to honor King Henri III of France, who was attending the christening of the fourth child of his grand provost, François du Plessis sieur de Richelieu. But the words on the banner held a deeper meaning; they accurately foretold the future of the infant, Armand-Jean du Plessis de Richelieu, who would grow up to become first minister of France and who would dedicate his life to the service of King Louis XIII.

Armand, the future Cardinal Richelieu, was born on September 9, 1585, in the Paris parish of St. Eustache, on the right bank of the Seine. His father was the grand provost at the court of Henri III; he functioned as the king's private police chief, enforcing discipline and loyalty in Paris and seeing that the king's edicts were obeyed. François — loyal, discreet, and violent when he needed to be — was the right man for the job. Armand's mother was Suzanne de la Porte, the daughter of a respected

Marie de Médicis, queen mother of France. After the assassination of her husband, King Henri IV, the queen mother adopted a conciliatory policy toward the Hapsburgs — a policy that the cardinal despised.

In 1615, on the Pyrenean frontier, in a ceremonious exchange of royal child brides, Madame Elizabeth, eldest daughter of France (background, left) was given to the Infante Don Philip of Spain (background, right), while the Infanta Anna, eldest daughter of the king of Spain, was given to Louis XIII, boy king of France.

and wealthy Parisian lawyer. Armand was the third son and the fourth of six children born to the grand provost and his wife.

For a period immediately following Armand's birth, his family worried that he might never have the chance to serve his king at all. The baby was tiny and sickly, but with the help of a peasant wet nurse from Poitou he survived. His health improved somewhat in his first years, but although he was an energetic — and even at times overactive — little boy, he remained delicate and was susceptible to illness for the rest of his life.

When Armand was but 5 years old, his father, who was 42, died. The death of François du Plessis was a blow to the Richelieus. Despite the money he had inherited from his own father, the dowry he had received from his wife's family, and the bonuses that came with his work, François du Plessis had never handled money well. To make matters worse, he had gambled, kept a mistress, and left enormous debts when he died. His widow was left to manage the household on a shoestring budget. Unable to maintain the house in Paris, she and the five children moved into her mother-in-law's château in Poitou.

As was usual in noble families of the time, the male children's future occupations were already established. The eldest son, Henri, would inherit the family estate — the seigneury of Richelieu — and was preparing for a life at court. The second son, Alphonse, was destined for the church and had been nominally bishop of the town of Luçon from the age of 12; the Luçon bishopric had been granted to the Richelieus by Henri III as a reward for François's loyal service, and now, with François dead, it represented the main source of income to the Richelieus. The third son, Armand, would be a soldier, and he was groomed for this career from the beginning. He was taught Latin by a local priest, and by the age of nine he was an accomplished horseman. At the age of 12, his mother enrolled him in the prestigious Collège du Navarre, where Armand excelled in his studies and was soon promoted to the leading military academy in France, run by Antoine du Pluvinel.

Armand was to spend most of his adolescence at the academy, and it was during this period that he blossomed intellectually, physically, and socially. He began to demonstrate uncanny powers of concentration and memory, and he quickly mastered all the subtleties of court etiquette required of a young cavalier. Armand also displayed considerable martial skills, and by the time he was 17 all his instructors and peers agreed that young Richelieu had a brilliant career ahead of him.

God's will be done.
—RICHELIEU
on learning that he must replace his brother as bishop of Luçon

The Luxembourg Palace in Paris, site of the queen mother's private quarters, was infiltrated by Richelieu on the night of November 30, 1630. The ensuing confrontation between the cardinal, the king, and Marie de Médicis is remembered in French history as the Day of Dupes.

It was at this point, in 1602, that fate stepped in. Alphonse, Armand's brother, suddenly announced that he would not assume the bishopric of Luçon, but that he intended to become a Capuchin monk instead. The widow Richelieu and her mother-in-law were appalled: The family could not afford to forfeit the bishopric, but if a Richelieu did not assume the position soon it would be lost to them. (It was currently held by a Richelieu designee who intended to retire.) Alphonse could not be dissuaded, Henri was destined for court, so there was no choice — Armand would have to forsake his military career for the ecclesiastical life.

Even at the age of 17, Richelieu's personality was formidable enough to make his mother dread telling him that he must sacrifice his military career. But her trepidation was unnecessary; her son accepted the news and made no protest. Instead he began packing his things and left the academy immediately. He withdrew to Poitou and began extensive theological studies. His family watched him for signs of resentment or frustration, but Armand was unperturbed. The goals he had already set for himself were not changed — he would simply have to arrive at them via a religious rather than a military path.

2

Who Will Be My Equal?

Shortly before he left the military academy to begin preparing for his new vocation as bishop of Luçon, young Richelieu wrote a Latin essay entitled "Quis Erit Similis Mihi?" or, "Who Will Be My Equal?" Richelieu was a serious young man, and he posed this question with complete sincerity. The nature of the question itself provides some insight into the personality of Richelieu at the age of 18. He had unbounded self-confidence and the ability to set a goal for himself and pursue it with total concentration. Perhaps this is why he was unfazed by the sudden change of careers that was forced upon him. For Richelieu, the church, like the military, was a system that could be analyzed and mastered. And, because of the deep involvement of the Roman Catholic church in European affairs of the time, it could serve him in the same way the military might have, bringing him to a position of power in France. Power was the ultimate goal. At 18, as far as Richelieu could tell, the answer to the question "Who will be my equal?" was "Nobody," and it seemed that there were no limits on how far the church might take him.

The rebuilt cathedral at Luçon, in western France, and the Luçon diocese itself were in disrepair when Richelieu assumed his bishopric in 1608, but both found new life under his ministry.

A 17th-century woodcut depicting the Catholic church tossed by the stormy seas of the Counter-Reformation. As bishop of Luçon, and later as first minister of France, Richelieu inherited the bitter results of a century of religious strife.

Richelieu set about the task of learning the ways of the Catholic church with concentration and tenacity. He withdrew from all social activity and sequestered himself in the family château among stacks of theological literature. He studied, virtually without interruption, for three years. The degree to which he dedicated himself to his theological studies does not indicate, however, an obsessional or mystical preoccupation with Catholicism, as was common at the time in Counter-Reformation Europe. From the first, Richelieu's association with Catholicism was pragmatic rather than spiritual, and it was to remain that way throughout his life. But, if he was to succeed within the Catholic church, it was necessary for him to master the subject of Catholicism in all its philosophical, metaphysical, and dogmatical complexity, and he did this with an astonishing speed and thoroughness.

By the end of his third year of study, the 21-year-old Richelieu was holding his own in debates with the British Jesuit Richard Smith, who was a renowned dialectician and, in the tradition of the Jesuits, a cunning debater and master of equivocation.

Although he was technically still too young to become a bishop, Richelieu decided to journey to Rome in an attempt to speed matters along. He made a great impression on the Catholic hierarchy of the Vatican, and the Vatican made a great impression on him. Richelieu was taken not so much with the people he met in Rome — including Pope Paul V — but rather with the place itself. Never had the young man seen such wealth and material splendor, even at the court of the French king in Paris. Such grandeur, Richelieu felt, added immeasurably to the atmosphere of power and supremacy exuded by the Vatican. The trappings of wealth, he decided, were essential to those who would assume and successfully wield authority over a populace that ranged from peasants to merchants to nobles; all classes of people respected wealth in 17th-century Europe. Gold and silver, silks and jewels lent an undeniable weight to the political and ideological heft of the church. As soon as he departed from Rome, Richelieu would begin — with the help of the church — to amass his own personal fortune. Let the Capuchins assume the threadbare mantle of Christ's poverty, if they so desired. For Richelieu, wealth, like his newly acquired knowledge of Catholic doctrine, was a political necessity.

The rulers of the Roman Catholic church were as impressed with Richelieu as he was with the gilded halls of the Vatican. Here was a young man with unlimited potential. He charmed them with the depth of his knowledge of Catholic doctrine, with his impeccable manners, and with feats of memory and concentration. The pope was amused, rather than offended, by Richelieu's bald-faced ambition, even when the young man lied to him about his age, claiming to be several years older than he actually was. The pontiff played along, and at the age of 22

Where the spirit of Catholicism had become lukewarm, they were the great revivalists.
—ALDOUS HUXLEY
on the Capuchins of the
Counter-Reformation

— 5 years under the required minimum age for bishops — Richelieu was ordained a priest and consecrated bishop of Luçon.

The young bishop now had a choice to make. Just because he was the bishop of Luçon did not mean that he actually had to go to Luçon and assume the rather mundane duties of a provincial bishop. The citizens of Luçon had not actually seen their bishop in 30 years. Instead, if he was so inclined, he could spend his time hanging about King Henri IV's court, where his brother Henri was already popular, and where he might, if he flattered the right royal personage, get himself appointed to a more prestigious position. Another young priest probably would have done so; Richelieu, however, decided to go to Luçon and take up his duties as bishop. He did this for two reasons: First, it would be the best way to become involved in church administration; and second, there was money to be had at Luçon — substantial revenue was generated by the lands attached to the benefice (an ecclesiastical office to which an endowment of land is attached).

Richelieu set out for Luçon in December of 1608. Initially, the new bishop must have regretted his decision. The weather was miserable, the roads were treacherous, and he was robbed during the journey. And he could not have been overjoyed upon arriving at his new home; Luçon was a dingy little town mired in the swamplands of western France. The official residence for the Luçon bishop was a decaying, drafty, and damp medieval edifice. The Catholic priests who were to serve under the new bishop were resentful of Richelieu's noble background, his youth, and his privileged position. The Catholics of the diocese regarded the church with cynicism and complacency, and the Huguenots, after the decades of bloody religious strife and persecution brought on by the Reformation, were as wary and hostile as ever. The bishop had his work cut out for him, and he immediately began the task of dragging Luçon out of the Middle Ages and into the present.

First things first: Remembering the lesson of

My house is my prison.
—RICHELIEU
on his tenure in Luçon

28

Rome, Richelieu began transforming the crumbling episcopal residence into a place that was fit for a bishop — after all, he was Rome's representative. He wanted to make it into an object of respect and admiration for the people and the priests of the diocese rather than a symbol of decay and dissolution. He hired men to repair the building, ordered various items from Rome — such as new silverware for the table and fine new vestments for himself — and took on a majordomo to put the house in good order and keep it that way. Soon the residence had acquired an air of discreet affluence, with the tall, elegant bishop, always fastidiously courteous and properly grave, moving purposefully about the halls. As Richelieu had hoped, the citizens of Luçon began to regard the local chapter of the Catholic church with a new respect.

With his left hand, Martin Luther consigns Roman Catholic popes, cardinals, and monks to the mouth of the beast. With his right hand, he points the way to salvation through the crucified Christ, while those who have escaped damnation eagerly partake of the Sacrament of Holy Communion.

This 16th-century woodcut depicts the pope collecting money paid to the clergy by Catholics in exchange for indulgences — official forgiveness of their sins. To the adherents of the Reformation, the selling of indulgences symbolized the corruption at the core of the Roman Catholic church.

Once he had set his house in order, Richelieu began to do the same for his flock. He quickly won over the support of the people of Luçon — both Catholic and Protestant — by petitioning the authorities to lower the taxes imposed on the town. He also tended conscientiously to the spiritual well-being of his people. He made himself accessible, instituted a system of religious education for the unlearned, and traveled faithfully to all the parishes in his diocese, saying mass, hearing confessions, and seeing to the various social and spiritual needs and woes of the citizens of Luçon. Soon Luçon had become a model diocese, and both the royal authorities in Paris and the church authorities in Rome were receiving glowing reports about the young bishop Richelieu.

At the same time that he was rebuilding his diocese, Richelieu was busy keeping in step with the current trends in Catholicism and forging alliances with the other bright young Catholic minds of Europe. In the wake of the convulsions of the Reformation, the Catholic church was undergoing changes, which were part of what came to be known as the Counter-Reformation. The Reformation itself was the movement initiated by a young German monk, Martin Luther, at the beginning of the 16th century. Disillusioned by the spiritual and political corruption of Christianity that was rampant in the Roman Catholic church at the time, Martin Luther and his followers began a movement of reform. The resistance of the established church to these reforms resulted in the secession of Luther and his followers from the Roman Catholic church, and as the Reformation spread across Europe, the Catholic church was split in two, with the adherents of reform establishing what came to be known as Protestantism.

A century of turmoil and religious war ensued, as each side attempted to gain political and spiritual supremacy in Europe. In some countries, such as England and Denmark, the Reformation triumphed. In others, such as Spain and Italy, it was crushed and, under the terrible eye of the Inquisition, never allowed to regain a foothold. In countries such as France, an uneasy truce held sway. By the early 17th century, the Protestants were firmly entrenched — although in certain places still under a state of psychological and social, if not military, siege — in much of France. Known as Huguenots, they had won a degree of freedom after a half century of often savage warfare with Catholic forces. The Edict of Nantes, passed in 1598, had ensured the Huguenots freedom of worship and full citizenship. But there was still a simmering animosity between the Roman Catholics and the Protestants of France.

The Reformation was followed by the Counter-Reformation, which was still in full bloom during Richelieu's time. This movement combined a spirit of reform within the Catholic church with attempts to halt the spread of Protestantism and to win "heretics" back into the fold of Roman Catholicism. One aspect of the Counter-Reformation was the appearance of individuals and new religious orders that were dedicated to a more spiritual Catholic devotion and, in some cases, to a mystical fervor toward the teachings of Christ. This revival was flourishing during Richelieu's years at Luçon, and he was careful to establish strong ties with these people, known as *les dévots*, shrewdly recognizing that they were on the verge of becoming the most powerful ideological faction within the French Catholic church.

Among the dévots were such men as the learned Father Bérulle of Paris and such orders as the Daughters of Calvary, founded by the nun Antoinette d'Orléans; the Carmelites of St. Theresa, founded in Spain; and the reformed Franciscans, the Capuchins, the order that Richelieu's brother Alphonse had joined. The most prominent and powerful French Capuchin was François le Clerc du Tremblay, commonly known as Father Joseph. Fa-

François le Clerc du Tremblay, Father Joseph, a product of the Counter-Reformation, was a Capuchin mystic who became Richelieu's political henchman.

By the age of 25, Richelieu had established himself as the most dynamic representative of the Catholic church in France, and he began to look for an opportunity to move into the higher circles of power.

ther Joseph was a mystic and a zealot who wanted to revive the Holy Wars against the Turks; he was to become Richelieu's right-hand man once the bishop had risen to power.

Although Richelieu was quick to establish alliances with the dévots, he was not so quick, while he was at Luçon, to assume their hard-line stance toward the Huguenots. For Richelieu, the bottom line was political expediency; there were times when he would need the Huguenots and times when he would want them out of the way. Richelieu was no mystic or zealot, like Father Joseph; his actions were not determined by the teachings of Christ or by some aspect of Catholic dogma — they were determined by expediency. Richelieu was always willing to do what had to be done in order to achieve his ends. While he was at Luçon, there was no political reason to antagonize the Huguenots; because it would serve no practical purpose, the bishop did not bother. However, his relationship with the dévots and the Huguenots was to play a major role soon enough.

33

King Henri IV is knifed by the assassin Ravaillac in Paris, May 14, 1610. The murder of the popular Henri was a tragedy for France, but it proved to be a stroke of good fortune for Richelieu.

Despite his success at Luçon, it was not long before Richelieu began to get restless. His ambition was like a constant thirst, and it had to be quenched. In 1610, he thought he saw a chance to drink deeply when French king Henri IV, on his way to attack Hapsburg forces on France's northeast frontier, was assassinated by the Catholic fanatic Ravaillac, who the Spanish had recruited to do the deed. Richelieu saw the tragedy as a way to catch royal ears, and he wrote a "condolence" letter of a most sycophantic nature to the widowed queen regent, Marie de Médicis, who was known to be sus-

ceptible to flattery. But Richelieu's brother Henri and some of his friends advised the bishop not to send the letter, which was, according to them, painfully obvious and unsubtle. Richelieu reluctantly agreed, recognizing that his ambition had overcome his better judgment. This, he vowed to himself, would never happen again. It would be five years before he had another chance to attract the royal attention. The bishop passed the time in Luçon, building up his personal finances and his political connections. When his second chance came, in 1615, he was ready.

3

The Boy-King

France as a whole was badly shaken by the murder of the popular Henri IV in 1610. His son, Louis XIII, the rightful Bourbon heir to the throne, was only eight years old when the assassination occurred. Louis's mother, the Italian-born Marie de Médicis, was appointed regent to rule in his place until he was deemed old enough to assume the crown himself. The queen mother was soon surrounded by the adventurers, manipulators, and predators who recognized the vulnerability of the French crown, now in the hands of a vain old woman and a sulking preadolescent.

Although it was Spain that was ultimately responsible for the assassination of her husband, the king, one of the queen mother's first actions as regent was to make peace with the Spanish. This was perhaps a wise decision; France had been weakened by internal religious and political strife, and Marie de Médicis wanted to avoid a confrontation with her powerful neighbor. Members of the dévots who had

Make the king absolute in his kingdom in order to establish order therein.
—RICHELIEU
on absolutism

The boy king of France, Louis XIII, became king at the age of eight, following the assassination of his father. Recognizing the weakness of the French crown, political predators swarmed to the royal court in Paris. Among them was Richelieu.

In 1615, Richelieu was chosen to compose and present the official address of the Estates General to the throne. Intent on taking advantage of this opportunity, he penned an artful and self-serving speech.

insinuated themselves into the queen mother's circle — the royal family was Catholic at this point, although Henri IV had been alternately Protestant and Catholic, depending on which best suited him politically — also advised against going to war with Spain because Spain was the major Catholic power in Europe, and a united Catholic front was necessary if the Protestants were to be rolled back in France and elsewhere. The Vatican had yet to give up its dream of a united Catholic Europe.

In 1615, in a ceremony held on the Pyrenean frontier, Spain was pacified by an exchange of royal brides: Princess Elizabeth of France was given to Prince Don Philip of Spain, and Princess Anne of Spain was pledged to the boy-king Louis of France. By accepting these matches, the queen mother, in effect, bowed to the superior power of Spain before the watchful eyes of all Europe. France had been relegated to playing the part of a weak sister to Spain.

In western France, the bishop of Luçon followed these events closely. Like a wolf stalking wounded prey, Richelieu sensed the weakness and disarray of the French leadership, and he waited impatiently for a chance to take advantage. In 1615 his opportunity came when the queen mother summoned the Estates General — France's representative body — to Paris in order to appease the populace, who were in a perpetual ferment, by letting them have their say. The three classes of the Estates General were the First Estate, the clergy; the Second Estate, the nobility; and the Third Estate, known as the commons, comprised of nontitled landowners, merchants, and craftsmen, who would eventually come to be known as the bourgeoisie, or the middle class. (The peasants had no representation.)

Richelieu, by now considered one of the preeminent members of the Catholic clergy in France, was chosen to compose and present the official address of the Estates General to the throne. Here was an opportunity that he did not intend to waste. Richelieu's address to the queen mother and her court was a masterpiece of veiled self-promotion. The bulk of the speech combined an in-depth assessment of the social and political situation in France with blatant flattery of the regent. The bishop offered various solutions to the problems France was faced with, but the one he harped on most noticeably was his suggestion that members of the clergy be given more power in matters of state. Catholic priests, Richelieu asserted, were especially suited to high office, for they were learned, loyal, and prudent, and, more importantly, he argued, they had no interest in such things as sex and the accumulation of wealth, which so often corrupted others who held positions of power. (Within 10 years, Richelieu would be one of the richest men in France.)

Richelieu's speech had the desired effect. Marie de Médicis was impressed with the bishop of Luçon, and she decided he could be a valuable ally and servant. She began to make use of him as her personal agent in various political affairs, and Richelieu embarked on an extended campaign of flattery, which

If France were for sale, they would buy France from France itself.
—RICHELIEU
on the friends of the queen mother

A gathering of the Estates General in Paris. Richelieu used the 1615 convening of France's representative body to court the favor of Marie de Médicis.

he aimed at the regent's well-known vanity about her own beauty and desirability. Soon he was named ambassador to Spain. The queen mother changed her mind at the last minute, however; she preferred to have the bishop at her side, so she named him minister of foreign affairs, and Richelieu assumed his place on the council of state.

Richelieu felt that he had finally attained the position of authority he had craved for so long, but he soon learned that the corridors of power in France were tortuous and mazelike — a single misstep could result in exile, imprisonment, or the summary loss of one's head. And Richelieu had attached himself to a star that was about to fall from the sky.

Following the murder of her husband and her assumption of power in France, Marie de Médicis had filled her court with friends, hangers-on, and sycophants. Her two favorites were her foster sister, Leonora Galigai, and Leonora's husband, Concino Concini. By 1617 these two shameless Italian opportunists, with the approval of the queen mother, virtually ran France, playing at king and queen and at the same time embezzling large sums of money, gold, and jewels from the royal coffer. Leonora often appeared in public sporting the crown jewels. There was already a considerable amount of resentment built up among the nobles and the Parisian populace toward Marie de Médicis because she was a foreigner and because of her policy toward Spain, and the behavior of her two Florentine friends added fuel to the flame.

A conspiracy, centered around the boy-king Louis, was hatched by the master of the horse, Luynes — who had become a father figure to the unhappy young Louis — and the captain of the king's guard, the Baron de Vitry. On April 24, 1617,

On April 24, 1617, Concini, the Florentine adventurer who acted as the queen mother's prime minister before Louis XIII came to power, was shot down on the steps of the Louvre by the captain of the king's guard.

Leonora Galigai was a political opportunist like her husband, Concini. Following Louis's assumption of power in 1617, she was executed as a witch.

Luynes, with the approval of Louis, ordered the murder of Concini. The Italian was shot down by the Baron de Vitri outside the Louvre. The queen mother was placed under house arrest, and Leonora Galigai was arrested and imprisoned. (Louis had her burned as a witch in July.) Turmoil swept through the Louvre. Louis XIII, now 16 years old, climbed on top of a billiard table, and as the cheering courtiers gathered about him, he shouted happily "I am king now! I am your king!"

The fall of the Concini ministry placed the bishop of Luçon in a precarious position. He was a member of the queen mother's cabinet and therefore he was perceived as one of Concini's supporters. He had gotten wind of the plot against Concini beforehand, and had hedged his bet by cultivating Luynes, in case the conspiracy succeeded. But Luynes did not trust Richelieu, and following the assassination of Concini, several of the bishop's colleagues were caught up in the purge and found themselves in the Bastille. Richelieu was clearly in jeopardy.

On the day after the killing of Concini, Richelieu, traveling through Paris by coach, came upon an irate crowd of Parisians, who, in the grand tradition of French mobs, had stolen the corpse of Concini and were tearing it limb from limb. The coach was quickly surrounded and forced to come to a halt. Angry faces peered into the coach. Was not this the bishop Richelieu, one of Concini's men? Richelieu, forced to improvise, complimented the mob on their handiwork and then led the crowd in a few rounds of "Long live the king!" Satisfied with the bishop's show of loyalty, the mob went back to its grisly business and a relieved Richelieu drove on.

Louis and Luynes were now firmly in control. Marie de Médicis was banished to the town of Blois, in north-central France, and with her, Richelieu. This was a bitter setback for the bishop; all his planning had come to naught. He remained with the queen mother, acting as a spy for Luynes and Louis in the hope of winning their favor and trust, but to no avail. Deciding that it would be best to disassociate himself somewhat from the queen mother, Richelieu returned to Luçon in 1617.

Richelieu remained in exile for seven years, and this was the most frustrating period of his life. Luynes quickly revealed himself to be nearly as corrupt as Concini, and the teenage Louis was moody and indecisive. As Richelieu fumed and plotted in Luçon, the decline of France continued, while Spain grew steadily stronger. Perhaps the only productive aspect of Richelieu's exile was that it allowed him the time to develop and finalize the political theory and the foreign and domestic policy that he would eventually employ to effect the return of France to Europe's cultural and military vanguard.

After he was assassinated, the hated Concini's corpse was horribly mutilated by an enraged Parisian mob. Richelieu escaped a similar fate by loudly proclaiming his loyalty to the king.

Following the purging of Concini and Leonora Galigai, Louis XIII, still a boy at age 16, strides triumphantly from the Château de Blois, followed by courtiers and his loyal guard. Young Louis's need for a trusted friend and adviser was eventually filled by Richelieu.

Richelieu believed that the main internal problem of France was a crisis in leadership. The idea of a "king" of France had become something of a joke to the other European powers. France, like many of the countries of Europe at this time, was less a nation or state than a loose association of republics, principalities, duchies, baronies, electorates, palatinates, and vassal states. The noblemen who ruled over these specific territories were often haughty and arrogant, resented the king, and considered themselves and their lands autonomous. Many of them maintained their own personal armies. In the past, for one reason or another, it was not unusual for a French nobleman to ally himself and his army with a foreign power in a war against the French king. Varying familial and religious loyalties only complicated the situation further. Richelieu correctly surmised that if France was to become a great power in Europe, the nobles would have to be brought into line and all authority would have to be consolidated in the king. This theory, known as political absolutism, was to be the cornerstone of Richelieu's domestic policy once he returned to power. Along with the establishment of an absolute monarch in Europe, he believed that the religious problem had to be solved and that Spain and the Hapsburg forces, which encircled France, must be checked.

Slowly, step by step, the way to Paris was reopened for Richelieu. He was maneuvering himself back into a position where he could put his theories into practice, but it was a slow, painstaking process. The main obstacles were Luynes, who still did not — and indeed would never — trust Richelieu, and the other ministers on Louis's royal council, mostly old men left over from the rule of Henri IV, who were jealous of the bishop and correctly recognized that they would be eclipsed if he won a place on the cabinet.

Luynes was removed as an obstacle when he died in 1621, and Richelieu scored points with Louis by twice dissuading the vengeful queen mother from leading the discontented nobility in revolts. He removed her as a threat to Louis by cleverly negotiating a reconciliation between mother and son. The queen mother returned to Paris, where Louis could keep an eye on her, but Richelieu remained in Luçon. The bishop had hoped that his diplomatic efforts would win him a place on the king's council, but the first minister, the elderly La Vieuville, talked the king out of calling Richelieu to Paris. Instead, as a reward, Louis asked the Vatican to make Richelieu a cardinal, and Rome was happy to acquiesce.

By 1624, Richelieu had allies in Paris who were too powerful for La Vieuville and the other ministers to resist. Agents of the pope — including the Capuchin Father Joseph — whose mouths watered at the idea of having one of their own on the king's council, campaigned steadily for Richelieu. And Marie de Médicis, who still believed that the cardinal was her pawn, exerted her own motherly pressure. Finally, in the spring of 1624, the king summoned Richelieu and offered him a position on the royal council, and so began one of the most fateful relationships in the long history of France.

What loyalty to the King!
—RICHELIEU
addressing the mob that
was dismembering
Concini

4

The Cardinal and the King

Once Cardinal Richelieu had gained access to the king's royal council, it did not take him long to assert his dominance over it; he did not intend to relinquish his position in Paris again. Initially, his most immediate rival was Louis's current first minister, the ancient La Vieuville, a decrepit leftover from the court of Louis's father. Richelieu wanted to take dictatorial control of the royal council, and La Vieuville, being a creature of political ambition himself, recognized this. He attempted a number of ploys to reduce the cardinal's role on the council, but to no avail. Richelieu, at the same time, was working to dispose of the old man. He engineered a propaganda campaign against the first minister; pamphlets accusing La Vieuville of various crimes against the king were circulated; and on August 13, 1624, La Vieuville was arrested and thrown into the Bastille. Notice had been served; the cardinal would henceforth brook no opposition on the council, and those who dared cross him did so at their own peril.

His passion for the chase was merciless and he sometimes rode his horses to death.
—C. V. WEDGWOOD
historian, on Louis XIII

Louis XIII (foreground) and Cardinal Richelieu, at the head of the royal army, set out to lay siege to the rebellious Huguenot fortress of La Rochelle in 1627. Louis named the cardinal head of the royal council in 1624, and, in war or peace, Richelieu was never again far from the king's side.

Richelieu wasted little time once La Vieuville was out of the way, and on August 24 he was appointed head of the royal council. At age 39, he now held the highest political office in the land; he was finally in a position to help his beloved France. It was time to take stock. France was in a pathetic condition, weak militarily and politically, surrounded by enemies, and wracked from within by religious strife and the endless intriguing of the nobility, who despised the king and were not above allying themselves with foreign powers or stirring up the Huguenots. The cardinal's work would be difficult,

Anne of Austria, queen of France. The willful Anne was related to the Hapsburgs, and her presence in court represented a threat to Richelieu. The king's inability to control her was a continual source of annoyance — and sometimes danger — for the cardinal.

but his objectives were clear: The Huguenots had to be neutralized, the nobility had to be brought into line so the power of the king could be made absolute, and the military expansion of Hapsburg Spain had to be checked. Richelieu set out to realize these objectives with his characteristic single-mindedness and force of will. But first, before he could begin his plan to revive France, the cardinal had to make an ally of the king himself. Without the complete cooperation of Louis XIII, nothing could be accomplished.

Louis XIII, as kings — and young kings especially — tend to be, was difficult. He was 22 years old when Richelieu became head of his council of state. Louis was sullen and emotionally weak, the exact opposite of his much-admired father. He compensated for his weakness by indulging an innate streak of cruelty, which he usually directed toward animals but also, occasionally, toward men and women. He was paranoid, secretive, obsessive, spiteful, and something of a lout who behaved badly in public. His marriage to Anne of Austria had become a disaster; Anne's beauty and her passionate nature were simply too much for him to handle, and he neglected and avoided her.

But if Richelieu, an astute judge of character, recognized all these faults in the young king, he also saw positive attributes. In the face of physical danger, Louis was fearless. He was highly intelligent; at times even brilliant. And, perhaps most important for the cardinal, Louis knew his own limitations, recognized good advice, and was not too proud to accept and use it when it was offered to him.

Richelieu cultivated his relationship with the young king with great care and even tenderness, employing all the powerful and subtle aspects of his personality to win Louis's trust and friendship. He became not so much a father figure to Louis, but rather a big brother; he was the king's confidant, comrade-in-arms, spiritual mentor, political adviser, and best friend. Louis, for his part, recognized that Richelieu was a great man and the most formidable ally he could hope to have — he needed the

> *Do you wish to make an end of duelling or of your own power?*
> —RICHELIEU
> to Louis XIII

The king's brother, Gaston, duke of Orléans, the lifelong nemesis of Louis and Richelieu. Known as "Monsieur," Gaston hated the cardinal, openly threatened to kill him, and plotted endlessly to overthrow him and the king.

cardinal. And once Louis accepted him, Richelieu became his lifetime servant; his devotion to the king was unshakable and unending. The two had a genuine liking for one another, but both men also seemed to realize that the future of France was inextricably bound to their relationship, and over the years they both worked hard to ensure its success, much like a couple who are determined to make their marriage a permanent one. The fruits of the marriage between the cardinal and the king would be many, although, in the long run, some would prove to be rotten.

Once he had secured the trust and support of the king, Richelieu began to assess France's domestic situation. The cardinal knew that he had to address France's internal difficulties before he attempted to tackle the situation abroad. In order to confront a power as formidable as Spain and its allies on the frontier, he must first deal with the problems within his own country — he would need a resolute and undivided France if he was to challenge the Hapsburgs.

Therefore, he turned his attention toward the two most divisive elements in France — the Huguenots and the French nobility. But he could not simply attack the nobles or the Huguenots outright; they were his countrymen, after all, and in the interests of future relations with Protestant powers abroad and the French citizenry, he would need some kind of provocation before he could move. He did not have to wait long: The nobility and the Huguenots were quick to provide Richelieu with the excuses he needed to take action against them.

No sooner had Richelieu taken control of the royal council than the first of many plots against his life was under way. The king's brother, Gaston, duke of Orléans, was the culprit. Gaston hated Richelieu, and over the years he was to become the cardinal's archnemesis. His very existence represented a threat to the cardinal; he was the successor to the throne if Louis died, he was openly hostile to the cardinal and had already threatened to knife him, and if he actually became king, there was no question that Richelieu would be his first victim. Gaston was not ready to wait around for his brother to die, however: In the summer of 1626, Richelieu's agents uncovered a conspiracy involving Gaston; two of the many bastard sons of Henry IV; Madame de Chevreuse, the beautiful and alluring best friend of Queen Anne; and one of Chevreuse's lovers, a starry-eyed young nobleman named Chalais. The plotters were quickly apprehended and dealt with. Of the five instigators, only the unfortunate Chalais was executed; to the cardinal's chagrin, the others received pardons because of their connections to the royal family. But Richelieu found another way to strike back at the nobility. Shortly after breaking Gaston's plot, he prevailed upon the king to pass a law prohibiting dueling on pain of death.

Dueling was the bloody but fashionable hobby of the hot-blooded young nobles of France. Despite its illegality, idle firebrands were constantly meeting at dawn and hacking away at one another over some trifling insult or imagined offense. Richelieu saw dueling as a highly public symbol of the nobility's

A duelist is run through by his adversary's sword. Richelieu felt that the nobility's penchant for public dueling was a symbol of their contempt for the king's laws, and he prevailed upon Louis to ban the practice. Those who ignored the king's ban were executed.

contempt for law and order and for the king's rule, and for this reason he persuaded Louis to impose the new law. It was quickly challenged by one of the most notorious duelists of Paris, the dashing and highborn Montmorency-Bouteville, who had killed 22 men in duels. Bouteville scoffed at the new edict and fought a duel in broad daylight in a Paris courtyard. To his own amazement, Bouteville was quickly arrested, tried, and then executed, despite the outcry from the noble families of Paris to spare the high-spirited young fellow. The message was clear: Louis was king, and those who did not obey his laws would suffer the consequences, no matter what their surname happened to be. Baronial independence had been dealt a symbolic blow.

Having won this first skirmish with the nobility, Richelieu's attention was quickly drawn to the second internal threat — the Huguenots. France's Protestant population had been understandably nervous about Richelieu's proximity to the seat of power in their country, and they were appalled to see him actually take control of it. A nominally Catholic king was one thing; but a high-ranking officer of the Vatican in control of the royal council was another matter entirely. Grim memories of the St. Bartholomew's Day Massacre — a royally sanctioned Catholic pogrom against the French Protestants in 1572 — still lingered, and soon agents of Protestant England, France's eternal enemy, were moving among the Huguenots of France, stirring up their resentments and fears, and sowing the seeds of a Huguenot uprising that would accompany an English invasion.

Among the horrors of Europe's Wars of Religion was the St. Bartholomew's Day Massacre of 1572, in which French Catholics slaughtered Huguenots by the thousands. Once Cardinal Richelieu came to power, the uneasy peace between France's Huguenots and the state did not last long.

The "royal flotilla" of 1627 was actually a hastily improvised armada of French commercial vessels. When the fleet proved too scanty to blockade the Huguenot fortress of La Rochelle, the cardinal and Louis built a gigantic dike across the harbor.

By July 1627, the masts and sails of an English naval force were bristling off the shores of the port city of La Rochelle, a Huguenot stronghold in western France. Upon seeing the fleet, the Protestants of the city rebelled and La Rochelle was quickly transformed into an armed Huguenot fortress. Concurrent Huguenot uprisings took place in the southern provinces. The cardinal now had the excuse he needed to step on the Huguenots, and he and Louis were undaunted by the presence of the English fleet, even though France had no true navy of its own. A makeshift fleet was raised, and, with Louis himself in command, they bore down upon the English, who quickly lost their nerve and withdrew, leaving the Huguenots of La Rochelle to their own devices.

The citizens of La Rochelle were defiant, and they settled in for a siege, confident that an English fleet would return. The French forces could not take the town by land, and they did not have enough ships to blockade its harbor. If the English did return, Richelieu realized, they would be able to land ships and reinforce La Rochelle. The cardinal, however, was determined to break La Rochelle, just as he had broken the duelists of Paris.

One morning in November, the besieged citizens of La Rochelle awoke to find that some kind of massive construction project had been started in their harbor. As winter approached, they watched from the walls, astonished at what they were seeing. Slowly, day by day, a gigantic structure took shape, rising behemothlike out of the gray waters of the harbor. Thousands of Frenchmen toiled in the cold and wet, swarming over the structure like vigilant ants. At times even the figures of Richelieu and the king were visible, the cardinal bizarrely attired in high boots, a huge red hat with plumes, and an armor breastplate over his scarlet robes, which were whipped in the wind and sea spray as he shouted instructions and orders while the king toiled happily with a pickax among the laborers and soldiers. Every morning the people of La Rochelle awoke to find that the great dam had grown a little higher and crept a little farther across the wide harbor, and every morning they looked at one another and wondered what kind of Catholic devilry this was.

The great dike of La Rochelle was the unlikely brainchild of Louis and Richelieu, the product of an inspired moment of speculation between the two. Unable to cut La Rochelle off from the British fleet by blockading the harbor with ships, they had wondered if a wall of masonry could be built across the harbor's entrance. By the time the English fleet reappeared in the spring, speculation had become reality. Dismayed by the uncanny feat of engineering that confronted them upon their return to La Rochelle, the English turned around and sailed for home. The Huguenots held on for several months more, but by October they had had enough. The triumphant king, flanked by the ever-present cardinal, entered La Rochelle on November 1, 1628. The most powerful symbol of Huguenot defiance in France had been broken.

So long as they have foothold in France, the King will not be master in his own house and will be unable to undertake any great enterprise abroad.
—RICHELIEU
on the Huguenots

The momentum generated by the victory at La Rochelle brought several more triumphs for Richelieu and Louis. While the Huguenot rebellion in the south was being crushed by the warlike duke of Condé, Louis and Richelieu marched their small but increasingly confident army to northern Italy, where their former ally, the duke of Savoy, had defected to the Hapsburg camp with his strategically important territory. The French forces crossed the Alps in March 1629, retook the territory, and the king, having sufficiently chastised the duke of Savoy, re-

Cardinal Richelieu stands defiantly atop the great dike of La Rochelle and watches the British fleet. The British, unnerved by this feat of engineering, gave up their attempts to relieve the besieged La Rochelle and sailed for home.

turned home. Back in Paris, Richelieu successfully parried two power plays by the queen mother, the second of which resulted in the Day of Dupes, the permanent banishment of Marie de Médicis from Paris, and Louis's naming of the cardinal as "principal minister of state." As 1630 drew to a close, Richelieu's position was as secure as it would ever be: He had broken the Huguenots, cowed the nobility, and parlayed his political influence into a vast personal fortune. He began to turn his attention outward, to France's uncertain borders and beyond.

5

Secret Treaties

It is necessary to have a perpetual design to arrest the progress of Spain, and while this nation has for its goal to augment its dominion and extend its frontiers, France should think only of fortifying herself, and of building bridgeheads into neighboring states to guarantee them against the oppression of Spain if the occasion should arise."

So wrote Cardinal Richelieu in 1630, defining what would be the guiding principle of his foreign policy for the remainder of his years as first minister of France. He hoped to build up the armed forces of France, creating a national army and, more importantly, a national navy; he would attempt to make allies of the various states that bordered France; and, ultimately, he would try to put an end to Hapsburg-Spanish domination of central Europe.

The prisons are full of the king's truest friends. The whole country groans under the tyranny of an arrogant churchman.
—GASTON, DUKE OF ORLÉANS
on France under Richelieu

Gustavus Adolphus II, king of Sweden (1594–1632). Gustavus was a Protestant, but what mattered more to Richelieu was the Swedish king's military prowess and his loyal and battle-hardened army. Because France could not yet field an army of its own, the cardinal hired Gustavus to fight for him in the Thirty Years' War.

Ferdinand II of Austria, the Holy Roman Emperor. Ferdinand was a Catholic who had the support of the Vatican, but more important for Richelieu, he was a Hapsburg. In 1631, at the bidding of the cardinal, the army of Gustavus of Sweden invaded Germany and attacked the emperor's forces.

In 1618, the conflict that would come to be known as the Thirty Years' War had broken out in the kingdom of Bohemia (now western Czechoslovakia), when the fiercely Protestant Bohemians refused to accept the Catholic Holy Roman Emperor, Ferdinand II of Austria, as their king. Catholic Germany and Hapsburg Spain, in the name of the Holy Roman Empire, embarked on a crusade against Bohemia and its various Protestant allies, and thus began the war that would rage across Europe for 30 years.

For Cardinal Richelieu, despite the bloodshed and destruction it wreaked upon Europe, the Thirty Years' War was a godsend, an opportunity for France to establish itself as the major power in Europe at the expense of Spain and the Hapsburgs. This would require nimble political and military maneuvering on the part of Richelieu, however. Although he was a cardinal of the Catholic church, his priorities were with France from the start, and he realized immediately that in order to defeat Catholic Spain and the Hapsburgs in Germany, he would have to ally himself with their enemies — including the Protestant forces of Europe. Richelieu had no qualms about this, and, despite the protests of many of the dévots, by 1628 Europe had begun to witness the strange phenomenon of Richelieu suppressing the Protestants in his own country while at the same time courting Protestant powers abroad. This was an act of considerable political dexterity that perhaps could only have been carried off by the cardinal.

Richelieu, a master strategist, began a campaign of espionage and secret diplomacy well before France officially entered the Thirty Years' War. His spies and agents were abroad in Europe as early as 1628, establishing tentative alliances with such nations as Denmark and Sweden, Holland and Switzerland. In 1630, Richelieu dispatched the devious Capuchin, Father Joseph, into Austria to disrupt the Hapsburg campaign for a unified Catholic Germany. A frail fellow with the burning eyes of a fanatic, Father Joseph had developed a hatred for the Hapsburgs and Spain because they refused to support his wild plan for a new crusade against the

In 1631—32, from his seat of power in Paris, Richelieu brilliantly manipulated the events and shifting allegiances of the Thirty Years' War, striking a heavy blow to the Hapsburgs without shedding a drop of French blood.

Turks. Now, at the bidding of Richelieu, he became a cancer in the midst of the Holy Roman Empire, wandering the roads of Germany in sandals and a threadbare gray cassock, muttering prayers to himself and sowing the seeds of suspicion and dissent among the enemies of France. Because of the pope's high regard for him, Father Joseph was immune from harm in the Catholic cities of Europe, but in many of these cities he was about as welcome as the plague.

By 1630, Richelieu was ready to enter the Thirty Years' War in a more overt fashion. The military forces of France, however, were not: Despite the efforts of the cardinal and Louis, the French army and navy were still not large or experienced enough to challenge the might of Spain and the Holy Roman Empire. Unable to field his own army, Richelieu did the next best thing: He secured the services of the most effective European fighting force not allied to the Hapsburgs, which belonged to the Protestant king Gustavus Adolphus of Sweden.

The bold and brilliant Gustavus had been planning an invasion of Germany; he had the men he needed, but he did not have the money necessary for him to sustain an extended campaign outside his own country. Richelieu, with money he had extracted from the Huguenots as a punishment for their rebellions, offered to subsidize a Swedish invasion of Germany. Negotiations were initiated, and in January 1631 an agreement was reached. By spring, the fierce armies of Gustavus were on the march across northern Germany, and the Catholic forces were fleeing before them.

The domestic front, in the meantime, had been relatively quiet since the Day of Dupes. But in the summer of 1631, Gaston, that perennial thorn in the cardinal's side, was once again stirring up trouble. The king's brother, having secretly married the sister of the prominent duke of Lorraine, had succeeded in persuading the duke and Henri de Montmorency, the popular and influential governor of Languedoc, to join him in a revolt against the cardinal and Louis.

> *The trouble with Gustavus was that, being a military genius of the first order, he had been able to force his French allies to swallow doses of Protestantism far longer than is good for a Catholic stomach.*
> —ALDOUS HUXLEY

The public execution of Henri de Montmorency, governor of Languedoc, who had led, along with Gaston, a failed revolt against Richelieu and Louis. The gentlemanly Montmorency held no grudge against the cardinal; in his will, he bequeathed several valuable paintings to Richelieu.

The rebels raised a small army of nobles and mercenaries, and hoping to be joined in their uprising by the peasantry and other elements of the discontented nobility, they marched on Paris. Louis led the small but experienced core of the royal army — veterans of the siege of La Rochelle and the Italian campaign — to meet the rebels. The two armies clashed at Castelnaudary in the south of France, where the pro-Gaston forces were destroyed. Montmorency fought gallantly, sustained many wounds, and was captured; Richelieu had his best physicians attend to the rebellious gentleman, and they kept him alive just long enough for him to participate in his own public execution. The duke of Lorraine was spared, but his capital at Nancy was occupied by royal troops. Gaston, once again, went unpunished.

Anyone who openly opposed Cardinal Richelieu usually paid for it with his head. But because he was the king's brother, the foppish Gaston plotted against the cardinal with impunity.

While Richelieu was attending to matters in his own backyard, Gustavus of Sweden and his army were hacking their way across Germany. After obliterating the main force of Ferdinand II's army at the east German village of Breitenfeld in late 1631, the Swedes had virtually been unstoppable. When Richelieu finished dealing with the revolt of Gaston and Montmorency and turned his attention back to Germany in the fall of 1632, he found that Gustavus had overrun Germany and was now surging into the kingdom of Bavaria. The cardinal was pleased with the rout of the Hapsburg allies in Germany, but he was distinctly alarmed by the position of Gustavus. The charismatic Swede was now in control of all Germany, and although he had agreed with Richelieu not to persecute Catholics in Germany and not to invade neutral countries or potential allies of the French — such as Bavaria — he obviously intended to do what he pleased.

Richelieu was in a difficult position. His practice of employing Protestant allies in his war against the Hapsburgs was about to backfire. Gustavus was on the verge of declaring himself emperor of Germany and instituting harsh measures against the German Catholics. If this occurred, Richelieu would have to answer for it not only to the dévots and Rome but to all the Catholics of France and Germany. It was one thing for the cardinal to support anti-Hapsburg armies, but it was quite another for him to finance the persecution of Catholics and the establishment of a Protestant empire in Germany. Gustavus's invasion of Germany was fast turning into a Protestant crusade, and the willful Swedish king was ignoring all of Richelieu's entreaties to curb his advance into Bavaria. Richelieu had realized too late that he could not control Gustavus.

On November 16, 1632, the army of Gustavus clashed with Ferdinand's imperial army, under the command of Count Wallenstein, at the town of Lützen in Bavaria. The Swedish army carried the day, but Gustavus was killed in the field.

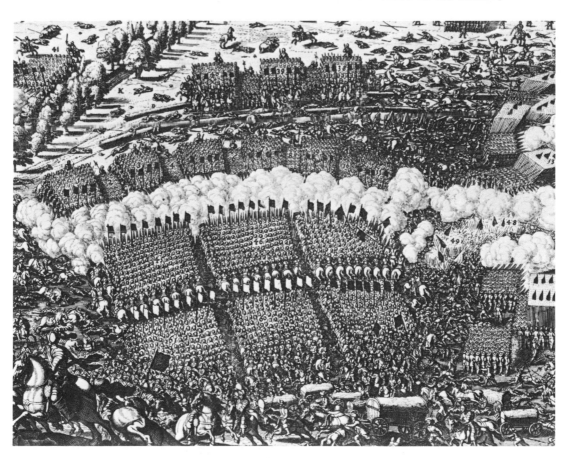

GVSTAVVS ADOLPHVS
D.G. SVEC.GOTH. ET VANDAL. REX, MAGNVS PRINCEPS
FINLAND. DVX ESTH. ET CARELIÆ, DOMINVS INGRIÆ. &c.

The death of King Gustavus at Lützen saddened all of Sweden and left his proud army in a demoralized state. Richelieu, however, welcomed the news; Gustavus had become too independent, and the cardinal feared that he could no longer control him.

A stroke of luck — in the form of the stroke of an Austrian sword — succeeded in doing what Richelieu could not: On November 16, 1632, the king of Sweden was killed on a battlefield in the Bavarian town of Lützen. When the cardinal heard this news, he offered a quick prayer of thanks to the Lord and then moved to regain mastery of the situation. With the loss of Gustavus, a power vacuum existed in Germany. The generals and rulers of the various Protestant German states gathered at the city of Heilbronn in March 1633 to address the situation. Richelieu sent one of his most effective diplomats, the marquis de Feuquières, to the conference to counter the influence of the Swedish chancellor Axel Oxenstierna, who had assumed control of the army of Gustavus.

The Protestant delegates to the convention established the Heilbronn League, an alliance against the Holy Roman Empire. Once the league was formalized, the conference became the scene of a contest between Oxenstierna and Feuquières for control of the league. Oxenstierna had the power of the Swedish army behind him, but he was quickly reminded by the French ambassador that without the financial support of France, that army would not be able to sustain its position in Germany. Oxenstierna had no choice but to allow the members of the Heilbronn League to sign a treaty with France that left the league beholden to Richelieu.

With the help of providence and his wily diplomats, Richelieu was once again in control of the situation in Germany. Through the use of the armies of other countries, he had managed to deal a serious blow to the Spanish-Austrian combine. He had used the shifting tides of the Thirty Years' War to his own benefit while at the same time keeping France unbloodied. In the late summer of 1634, however, the cardinal's remarkable tightrope act came to an abrupt end.

Following the death of Gustavus, Richelieu found himself casting about for a new leader to spearhead the fight against the Hapsburg forces. He found that leader in the bold German, Bernard of Saxe-Weimar.

In September 1634, a large and powerful Spanish army, under the leadership of King Philip III of Spain's brother, the Cardinal-Infante Don Ferdinand, launched an attack against the combined German-Swedish Heilbronn forces, under Marshal Horn of Sweden and the young German warrior, Duke Bernard of Saxe-Weimar. Despite the fighting prowess of the Swedish army and Saxe-Weimar, the Heilbronn forces were overwhelmed at the Bavarian commune of Nördlingen, near the Danube River. The core of the Swedish force remained intact, but the German armies scattered. After the rout, the victorious Spaniards marched on the Netherlands.

The ramifications of the disaster at Nördlingen were many. Richelieu quickly assured Bernard and Oxenstierna that they would not be abandoned by France, but the cardinal nevertheless hesitated from taking direct action against Spain. Everyone in Europe expected France to declare war on Spain.

On September 6, 1634, in one of the most important battles of the Thirty Years' War, an imperial army under the command of the Cardinal Infante Don Ferdinand of Spain fell upon the forces of the Heilbronn League at Nörd lingen in Bavaria. The Swedish-German army was overwhelmed and lost 17,000 men.

Louis XIII was all for it — he was always spoiling for a fight—but Richelieu waited.

Although he had spent the past 10 years preparing for a war with Spain by building up the French army and navy, securing the French borders, and forming alliances, the cardinal still harbored doubts about the ability of his countrymen to engage Spain in a true war. To lose a war with Spain now would mean the undoing of everything Richelieu had worked for since coming to power. By the spring of 1635, however, events conspired to force the cardinal's hand. Spanish troops were massing on France's borders, a Spanish armada was reportedly gathering for a foray down the French Mediterranean coast, and Spain's Catholic allies in Germany were pressing the last remnants of the Swedish and Heilbronn armies. Richelieu decided to act before he lost control of events completely, and on May 21, 1635, France officially declared war on Spain.

6

The Year of Corbie

Now that a state of open war existed between France and Spain, would the French be able to stand up to the mighty Spanish army and navy? There was still no French navy, realistically speaking. The French troops certainly looked good; there was no army more pleasing to the eye in drill or parade than the plumed, shining, colorful French army. But could they fight? How would the handsome French fare against *los tercios*, the renowned Spanish infantry? Could they endure the kind of grueling, extended warfare a Spanish invasion would bring? Richelieu had his doubts. In a letter to Louis on the subject, he wrote, "There is no people in the world less suited to war than ours. [Our] levity and impatience in the least hardship are two failings which, unhappily, put this proposition beyond all doubt. Although Caesar is said to have observed that the French understand two things, the art of war and the art of conversation, I must confess that I have yet to discover on what grounds he attributed the first of these qualities to them."

It was the goodliest sight that ever I beheld; they were all in bright armour and great feathers wonderful beautiful to behold.
—SYDNAM POYNTZ
British mercenary, on first encountering French troops

King Louis XIII goes to war with an image of Richelieu emblazoned on his shield. After the disastrous battle of Nördlingen, Richelieu was forced to declare war on the Holy Roman Emperor and Spain. The cardinal was not prepared for the ensuing invasion of France, but Louis was.

Because the soldiers of the French army were a dandified lot who paid more attention to their colorful uniforms than to matters of war, Richelieu feared they would not stand up to the vaunted Spanish regulars.

Richelieu's misgivings about his fellow Frenchmen were compounded by feelings that he might have maneuvered France into a tight corner. The situation was grim, and, the cardinal realized, it was partly his fault: He had antagonized Spain in an underhanded way for years and had finally brought its wrath down on the heads of his own frivolous and decidedly unwarlike countrymen. Richelieu had hoped to challenge the power of the Spanish empire at some point in the future. "States need war from time to time to expel their base humours," the cardinal had written, "to win back what is lawfully theirs, to requite affronts which, if they went unpunished, would provoke further affronts, to preserve their allies from oppression, to humble the conqueror." But France, Richelieu feared, was not yet strong enough to "humble the conqueror." Nor was the cardinal himself ready for war; it had come too soon.

As summer wore on to autumn, Richelieu's forebodings grew. Key positions on the French perimeter fell one by one to the Spanish and their Austrian allies; armed French resistance was flimsy at best, and frequently nonexistent. By winter, the armies of Spain and the Holy Roman Emperor were poised at the strategic Zabern gap in the Vosges Mountains bordering northeastern France. The enemy was knocking on France's back door.

The citizens of Paris settled in for a cold and jittery winter. Rumors of the imminent downfall of their country filled the air. Richelieu attempted to stanch the rising tide of panic by planting stories in the *Gazette*, a Paris newspaper and the cardinal's personal propaganda mouthpiece. In the *Gazette* that winter, every minor skirmish at the front became a major French victory. But the people were not deceived; everybody knew that the enemy was simply waiting for the spring. When the warm weather came, so would the Spanish.

The cardinal used what little time he had to strengthen the French defenses. He signed a treaty with the Italian dukes of Savoy, Mantua, Modena, and Parma, which complemented the three impor-

Holy Roman Emperor Ferdinand II of Austria, acting in concert with the Cardinal Infante Don Ferdinand of Spain, unleashed his murderous imperial army on France in the summer of 1636.

tant treaties he had signed previously, with Bernard of Saxe-Weimar, the Dutch, and the Swedes. And, using a Huguenot force, he managed to secure possession of the Val Telline, a key Alpine pass. But still the cardinal feared that France could not withstand a major offensive. When spring arrived, Richelieu, Louis, and all the French waited. The enemy made no move as spring turned to summer, but rather than giving France a moment of relief, the stillness only increased the suspense. Finally, in the heat of midsummer, the storm broke.

Like the invading army, the bad news came slowly at first, then in a great and seemingly unstoppable torrent: Enemy troop movements had been detected; 6,000 horsemen were advancing on the town of Clermont; a full-scale invasion was under way. It was a two-pronged assault, as Richelieu had feared. The Cardinal-Infante Don Ferdinand of Spain and the army he had brought to the Netherlands following the great battle at Nördlingen, and Count Gallas, with the imperial army, had linked up and were surging into northern France. The frontier garrison towns had been overrun and their defenders scattered, the countryside was in flames, and the people were fleeing to the hills and into the woods. Corbie, the last major fortress between the enemy and Paris, was threatened.

Richelieu's darkest hour was upon him — everything he had worked for was in dire jeopardy — and for what was probably the first time in his life, he lost his courage. Had he dedicated his life to France only to be forced to witness her ignominious demise? Had he served the Crown so faithfully, only to see Paris, the greatest jewel, fall into the hands of Spaniards and German mercenaries? He shouted and raved, gave orders and withdrew them immediately, sobbed uncontrollably and wailed prayers and recriminations to the Almighty. He was by turns furious and abject. He ordered the arrest of the three French commanders who had lost the town of Châtelet; he would have them dragged behind horses through the streets of Paris until they were dead. When the officers got wind of the cardinal's rage and fled, Richelieu had effigies created and dragged through the streets in their place.

While the cardinal was experiencing his breakdown, the enemy was advancing, heading straight for Paris, raping, pillaging, slaughtering the peasants, and putting the French countryside to the torch as they came. Terrified refugees poured into the city, hoping to find sanctuary behind its walls. Paris was safe, so everyone believed. But on August 15 came the dreaded news: Corbie had fallen. The way to Paris lay open to the enemy. In the streets

All their bravery which they showed at their coming was gone, we could see at their parting neither scarlet coats nor feathers, and they sneaked and stole away little by little.
—SYDNAM POYNTZ
on first encountering
French troops in battle

and in the staterooms of the great French city, panic now reigned. The Parisians began to flee westward, their belongings carried on horses or mules, piled in carts or strapped to their own backs. At night, the sky to the north was aglow, lit by the fires of war.

France, in its greatest hour of need, was rescued by a combination of people and events: King Louis XIII; Father Joseph; Bernard of Saxe-Weimar; the fatal hesitation of the cardinal-infante; and the French themselves. Had one of these elements been removed, the Spanish and Austrians would have marched into Paris in much the same manner as the Nazis three centuries later.

If the year of Corbie, as 1636 came to be known

Hapsburg forces converge on the French town of Corbie in August 1636. Corbie was the final obstacle between Paris and the oncoming Spanish and imperial armies. News that Corbie had been taken by the enemy reached Paris on August 15.

to the French, marked the cardinal's darkest hour,
it marked Louis XIII's finest. As Richelieu's resolve
crumbled, Louis's grew stronger. As his ministers
quailed and called for retreat, Louis stood fast. Perhaps he realized that here was his moment; his
chance to come out from under the shadow of the
cardinal, to justify his birthright and show what it
meant to be king of France. Perhaps he was simply
a man who possessed the qualities of courage and
leadership in grave and seemingly hopeless situa-
tions. Whatever the reasons, his response to the
crisis was kingly in every sense of the word.

As soon as the news that Corbie had fallen
reached Paris, Louis called his council into an emer-
gency session. The king examined the pale and hag-

gard faces of his ministers, including the cardinal,
and asked them, one by one, what should be done.
Paris should be abandoned, they told him. The king
and his court must withdraw beyond the Seine, con-
solidate their forces, and wait for a chance to retake
the city. Louis looked at the cardinal. Richelieu
agreed with the others: They must abandon Paris
to the invaders.

Louis, with quiet disdain, dismissed this advice
completely. Paris, he told the council, would never
be surrendered. The ministers listened in amaze-

Refugees flee Paris in the face of the oncoming Spanish-Austrian juggernaut. Panic and despair in Paris found its way from the streets to the royal palace; even Richelieu succumbed to hopelessness and dismay.

ment as the king, in a somewhat matter-of-fact manner, explained the course of action he would take. He would gather the staunchest members of his royal guard, mount his finest horse, and ride straight to Corbie, where he would rally the demoralized French troops and make a stand, holding off the invaders until Bernard of Saxe-Weimer arrived with reinforcements. This being said, the king went to make arrangements for his journey; he intended to leave for the front at once. His councillors were left staring at one another in shocked silence.

By nightfall, Louis was at the front, doing exactly as he had said. But unlike the soldiers who were rallying to their king, Richelieu did not take heart in the courage of Louis. Instead, his depression deepened. He believed that Louis's actions were fool-hardy; that they would prove disastrous; that France was now irrevocably doomed. In the streets, the mob was calling for the cardinal's head; they knew as well as Richelieu himself that his were the very policies that had brought them to the present deplorable state of affairs. In agony, Richelieu shut himself up in the Palais Cardinal, the magnificent home he had built in Paris.

Louis's reaction to the crisis was bold and deci-sive. Without the cardinal behind him, however, his

Louis XIII leads the French forces to a desperate stand at Senlis, on the outskirts of Paris. The heroic behavior of their king inspired the French, and the invading armies were halted just short of the French capital.

moment of greatness would flicker out all too quickly. If he was to stop the enemy advance, he would need support from Richelieu. The cardinal's administrative genius was essential at this time. If Richelieu could take control of the situation in Paris, calm the panicked ministers and citizens, effectively organize the flood of volunteers that were pouring into the city, eager to join the king in battle; in short, if the cardinal could reassume mastery of himself and the situation, there was yet hope for France. But in his present condition, he was useless to his country and his king.

It was at this point that Father Joseph, the ubiquitous Capuchin, diplomat, spy, saboteur, and holy man, arrived on the scene. In his worn sandals, his

Father Joseph attempts to console a distraught Richelieu. While King Louis was rallying the French troops at Senlis, the strange Capuchin was attempting to do the same for the cardinal.

plain gray vestments and hood, he shuffled unnoticed through the chaotic streets of Paris, moving against the outflowing stream of refugees, murmuring his incessant prayers. When he arrived at the Palais Cardinal, Richelieu was so overjoyed that he wept. Father Joseph quickly spirited the cardinal away to a private corner of the palace, where they remained, in deep conversation, throughout the night and into the early morning hours. The cardinal's problem, Father Joseph explained, was simply a lack of faith. Richelieu listened intently. And in its own strange way, Father Joseph's diagnosis was entirely accurate.

Richelieu, despite his title and cardinal's robes, was a pragmatic man; a man whose sensibilities were grounded in the material world. What faith he did have was placed in his own abilities, in treaties and diplomacy, in maps and documents, in the number of cannon on a man-of-war and the amount of gold in the royal treasury. Father Joseph, on the other hand, lived almost entirely in an abstract world. He behaved as if he had a direct hot line to Jesus Christ himself — many believed that he did — and his faith was based entirely on arcane mystical principles that only he could comprehend; thus, it was unshakable. In the present situation, where concrete reality was overwhelmingly negative, Father Joseph's faith was by far the more desirable. Only he could see victory in an advancing army of Spanish shock troops, in overwhelmed French defenses, in a ravaged countryside, in a threatened Paris. And only he, with his almost hypnotic powers of persuasion, could convince Richelieu, the realist, to see this victory also. For France, Father Joseph's presence in Paris that night was providential in more ways than one.

The exact words that the Capuchin used in his conference with Richelieu that night are not known, although the cardinal later revealed that along with the spiritual advice he offered, Father Joseph provided counsel of a more earthly nature: He admonished the cardinal for behaving like a "*poule mouillée*" — a wet hen. Whatever else it was that Father Joseph said, it worked. The next morning, to the astonishment of the Parisians, the cardinal appeared — unguarded — in the streets. Boldly, he had his coachman drive right into the center of the mob that only the night before had been more than ready to spill his blood. Impressed by this audacity, the people did not assault the cardinal. Instead, they listened quietly as Richelieu told them to stay calm, to have hope, to pray, and to remain in Paris to help the war effort. He exhorted all able-bodied men to enlist in the army. He was, once again, the model of superior confidence and composure, a man who was in complete control of the situation. Soon the crowds were cheering him as his coach rolled through the streets of Paris, and by nightfall the panic had subsided and a new feeling of pride in France and unity against the invader prevailed. Richelieu, tireless once again, returned to the palace and began working ceaselessly to organize for a counterattack against Corbie.

The people of France, for their part, matched the

For Richelieu, the friar was a living conduit, through which there flowed into his own soul a power from somewhere beyond the world of time and contingency.
—ALDOUS HUXLEY
on Father Joseph
and Richelieu

The Palais Royal in Paris. For Richelieu and France, 1636, the "Year of Corbie," began disastrously. But, as the year drew to a close, Paris and her treasures remained unmolested despite the fears of the cardinal.

valour of the king. Volunteers flooded into Paris, and soon Richelieu, at the head of a new army of 20,000, rode out to join Louis. The French, so disparaged by Richelieu for their lack of military prowess, fought valiantly and well in defense of country and king. And the cardinal-infante contributed to the French resurgence by making the grave mistake of hesitating. Had he pushed on in a concentrated attack against the city immediately following the capture of Corbie, he probably would have taken the French capital. Instead, against the urging of his top military advisers, Don Ferdinand halted the advance at Senlis, just outside the suburbs of Paris.

The momentum of his army's onslaught was bro-
Saxe-Weimar arrived with his battle-hardened
troops. Paris held. Louis, with the reinforcements,
laid siege to Corbie, and it was back in French hands
by early November. Harried by Louis and the men
of Saxe-Weimar, the two invading armies withdrew
from France before winter set in. The war was not
over; indeed, for France it was just beginning, but
the year of Corbie was a pivotal moment for France.
Whether from luck, courage, or divine providence,
defeat had been transformed to victory, and once
again, Cardinal Richelieu — and France — had
survived.

CCIOS, QVI FORTIBVS ARMIS

7

Red Eminence

Although the retaking of Corbie and the successful resistance to the Spanish-Austrian invasion marked an important victory for France, it by no means signified an end to the war. In fact, for France the war was just beginning, and hostilities would continue to disfigure the face of Europe for another two decades; the Thirty Years' War was to outlive both Richelieu and Louis XIII. The cardinal, recognizing that France was now committed to a protracted struggle, spent the final years of his life preparing his country for a long war of attrition.

Ever since the battle for La Rochelle, when French forces had been unable to blockade a harbor for lack of vessels, Richelieu had been determined to build a French fleet. He recognized that without a true navy, France could not defend her extensive coastlines from the Spanish armada or any future enemies, including the seaworthy English. A French fleet was also needed to protect coastal towns from the marauding Barbary pirates, who had been raiding the helpless fishing villages with virtual impunity for years.

> *With only a small force the Duke of Saxe-Weimar has achieved great things which other generals with large forces are unable to achieve.*
> —LOUIS XIII

Louis XIII is depicted being crowned by Victory, following the retaking of Corbie in 1636. The king and Richelieu hoped that the failure of the invasion of France would signal a quick and decisive end to the war against the Hapsburgs, but they hoped in vain; the war was to rage across Europe for 24 more years.

Cardinal Richelieu is borne from the ocean on Poseidon's chariot, in a painting representing the emergence of France as a naval power during the Thirty Years' War.

Richelieu had taken the most important step toward establishing a national navy back in 1629 when the edict known as the *Ordonnance de la Marine* was passed. The Ordonnance laid down the bureaucratic groundwork for the construction of a fleet and the establishment of a naval administration, and a military hierarchy, from admiral to ship commanders down to galley slaves. Under the watchful eye of the cardinal, the program progressed slowly but steadily, and by 1636 a formidable French fleet, under the command of Henri de Sourdis, the archbishop of Bordeaux, was patrolling the Atlantic and the Mediterranean.

The French navy came of age none too soon. The Spanish armada, upon the outbreak of hostilities with France, had seized the Mediterranean islands of Lérins, from which they launched assaults on the French coast. In May 1637, French ships engaged Spanish men-of-war in the waters off the islands. The Spaniards were driven away and the Lérins were once again in French hands. Following this encounter rumors about the new French fleet began to travel up and down the Mediterranean, but the French had still to prove themselves in a pitched naval battle with the Spanish. Their chance came in the summer of 1638, when a large Spanish fleet, intending to relieve the besieged Pyrenean fortress of Fuentarrabia, attempted to run a French blockade off the coast. The results were disastrous for the Spanish navy, which lost 17 ships in the fray and never fully recovered.

In the meantime, the land war on the Continent gradually developed into what was, for the average European commoner, a nightmarish affair. After the invaders had been driven from French soil in the year of Corbie, a period of desultory attack and retreat set in, with neither side gaining any real advantage. The French and their allies, under the leadership of Duke Turenne of Bouillon, Duke Condé, and the indefatigable Bernard of Saxe-Weimar, fought the Hapsburg forces on several fronts, in Germany, Italy, Flanders, and the Pyrenees. When the various armies were not fighting, they generally spent their time laying waste to the countryside, relieving the natives of all their food, and occasionally slaughtering them. Forests burned and towns were plundered. The plague broke out and there was widespread starvation. In some areas, after an army had swept through, the residents were reduced to cannibalism for lack of food.

Barbary, a region in North Africa, was a refuge for Arab and Turkish pirates who preyed on French shipping. Richelieu's navy succeeded in curbing the Barbary pirates' activities, which were halted for good when the French conquered Algeria in 1830.

Cofte de Barbarie

Tetoüan

GIBRALTAR

DE

In the spring of 1638 the situation began to change in favor of the French forces. Not surprisingly, it was the consummate mercenary Bernard of Saxe-Weimar who was responsible. After a period of inactivity, Saxe-Weimar and his private army embarked on a lightning march up the Rhine River. His objective was Breisach, a massive and supposedly impregnable fortress on the Rhine's east bank. Breisach was the seat of the Austrian monarchy in that region, and it was also of crucial strategic value; if the stronghold could be taken, Austrian domination of the Rhine would be broken and the Spanish line of communication with the rest of Europe severed.

The new French fleet first appeared in force near the Mediterranean Lérins Islands, where they encountered several Spanish warships. By the time of the cardinal's death in 1642, the French were vying with the Spanish and the Turks for control of the Mediterranean.

An imperial force was waiting to intercept Saxe-Weimar at Rheinfelden, just below Breisach, when he arrived in March. Saxe-Weimar's troops crushed the Austrians, and Breisach was surrounded. The fortress could not be taken by storm, so Saxe-Weimar and his troops settled in for a siege. In order to prevent reinforcements from breaking through the siege to relieve the fortress, Saxe-Weimar had a wall built around the outside of his own entrenched army, who in turn encircled Breisach — a tactic known as a Dutch siege. Trapped within this double ring, Breisach starved.

By winter, the desperate citizens of Breisach had eaten every horse, dog, cat, rat, and mouse within the city's walls, and as the holidays approached corpses were being snatched from the graveyards and devoured. No sooner had someone starved to death than he became his neighbor's dinner. Finally, just before Christmas 1638, the fortress on the Rhine capitulated. Richelieu was delighted, but his delight quickly turned to annoyance when Saxe-Weimar announced that instead of turning Breisach over to the French, he intended to keep it for himself. The great Bernard of Saxe-Weimar conveniently died shortly thereafter, however — many believed he was poisoned by the cardinal — and Breisach, as well as Bernard's proud army, who fought on with the French and came to be known as the Bernardines, were absorbed by France.

The victories of French forces at sea and on land marked a turning point in the Thirty Years' War. Soon, revolts against the Spanish crown in Portugal and Catalonia — orchestrated by Richelieu's secret service — further weakened the Hapsburg empire. Thereafter, France would slowly but steadily assume military dominance in Europe; Richelieu's dream of breaking the Hapsburgs and establishing the Bourbons as the ascendant European line was well on its way to realization. And, on the home front, the cardinal was handed another victory of sorts when Anne presented Louis with a baby boy — Louis XIV — in September 1638. The arrival of a direct heir to the throne reduced the cardinal's eternal nemesis,

Bernard of Saxe-Weimar, the last of the great *condottieri* (mercenaries of the Middle Ages), died suddenly in the summer of 1639. "I am surprised," he said moments before his death, "that my heart is still so fresh and will not resign itself to death."

Gaston, as a threat. If Louis XIII died, young Louis, instead of Gaston, would succeed to the throne, and the cardinal, and his policies after him, would survive.

The Red Eminence, as Richelieu was known throughout Europe — with varying degrees of respect and loathing — was now 53 years old, and his health, precarious for years, was failing rapidly. He knew that he did not have long to live. With the victories of the French armed forces abroad and the birth of the Dauphin at home, it would seem that Richelieu could now rest and enjoy some satisfaction in his accomplishments. But this was not to be so. It was easier for the cardinal to subdue his powerful foreign foes than it was for him to neutralize the more insidious domestic threats that continued to plague him, literally until the day he died.

Courtiers pay homage to Queen Anne and the dauphin, Louis XIV. The birth of the dauphin was a blow to Gaston, who would have assumed the throne if Louis XIII died without producing an heir.

The most serious and far-reaching of these domestic threats was the discontent of the masses. The cardinal needed funds to support his military ventures, and he acquired these funds through heavy taxation, the brunt of which fell squarely on the shoulders of the peasantry and the Third Estate. The taxes, along with the marauding armies that crisscrossed the countryside and stripped it of food, left the peasantry in a deplorable state. Gaston, the king's brother and the cardinal's harshest critic, accurately described the plight of France's peasant farmers in a public manifesto: "Beware of the pitiable condition to which France has been reduced by the Cardinal's ambition. . . . Today less than a third of the people living on the plains eat real bread. Some live on oats while others not only are reduced to begging but are in such misery that the greater part are dying of starvation. Those who survive do so on a diet of acorns, grass and the like, just like the beasts of the fields."

Such conditions gave rise to sporadic popular revolts during the early decades of the 17th century, and by the time France formally entered the Thirty Years' War, these uprisings were occurring with an alarming frequency. In 1636–37, peasant armies known as the *croquants* (biters) took to the streets and fields in a widespread spontaneous revolt that was eventually crushed by royal troops. On the heels of this insurrection came the uprising of the *Nu-Pieds* (bare feet) in Normandy, a loosely organized coalition of peasants named after a mythical, shoeless proletarian hero, Jean Nu-Pieds. The Nu-Pieds wreaked havoc in Normandy and won extensive popular support until they were cornered by a punitive force of 8,000 mercenaries hired by the king. Trapped against a small river near the town of Avranches, most of the peasants were driven into the water and drowned after a courageous but futile battle; those who escaped a watery death were captured and hung from nearby trees. The revolt of the Nu-Pieds was the last of the major popular uprisings during Richelieu's time, but the simmering discontent of the people would prove to be one of the most fateful and bitter legacies left to the future leaders of France by the cardinal.

There were others in France who were determined to give the cardinal no rest. Although Gaston had been weakened by the birth of the Dauphin, Richelieu was never out of danger; plotting against the cardinal was still the favorite pastime of the nobility, and there were even anti-Richelieu cabals among the dévots, who opposed the war against Catholic Spain and the Holy Roman Emperor.

The last plot against Richelieu developed early in 1642. The plot revolved around the 17-year-old master of the horse, Henri d'Effiat, Marquis de Cinq-Mars. Louis, who was prone to becoming involved in obsessional relationships, was infatuated with the youthful and arrogant Cinq-Mars. Cinq-Mars, who had no real affection for the king, took advantage of the situation to gain power and prestige in

What do you think you're up to?
—RICHELIEU
to Cinq-Mars

court. Louis fawned pathetically as the young man preened about Paris. Richelieu was confined to his bed because of his rapidly disintegrating health, but he could still smell a plot a mile away, and his spies kept him informed daily, and sometimes hourly, of the progress of the conspiracy. Despite the fact that he was the king's favorite, the unfortunate Cinq-Mars soon found that he was merely another fly in the cardinal's web.

To the young man's credit, he succeeded in building a conspiracy of considerable detail and scope. He was in touch with Spanish agents, Huguenot

The Thirty Years' War and the regime of Cardinal Richelieu left the peasantry of France in a deplorable state. Starving and destitute in a war-ravaged land, they frequently engaged in bloody uprisings.

elements, the rebellious duke of Bouillon, and, of course, Gaston. If everything went according to plan, Richelieu would be faced with a massive uprising on several fronts: Gaston would begin the revolt in the key fortress of Sedan; the duke of Bouillon would join Gaston with the entire French army in Italy, of which he was in command; and Cinq-Mars, according to a secret treaty he had signed with the Spanish, would be furnished with a Spanish army of 18,000. Various other anti-Richelieu elements among the nobles and the clergy would also participate.

The execution of Henri d'Effiat, marquis de Cinq Mars, December 12, 1642. The arrogant young man had the honor of being the last person sent to the chopping block by Cardinal Richelieu.

The coup would be set in motion by the assassination of the cardinal; Cinq-Mars knew that the success of his plan depended on the death of Richelieu. Unfortunately for Cinq-Mars and his fellow conspirators, Richelieu was perhaps the most well protected man in Europe at the time; it was easier to get to the king than it was to get to the cardinal, who existed at the center of a personal army of soldiers, spies, bodyguards, and secret agents of one kind or another. Richelieu had already survived numerous attempts on his life, and he survived this time as well, even though Cinq-Mars's assassins had two chances to dispatch him.

Shortly after the second attempt on his life, the sickly cardinal, bedridden amid hundreds of documents incriminating Cinq-Mars and the other

conspirators, sprang his trap. The duke of Bouillon, Cinq-Mars, and a number of others involved in the plot were apprehended; Gaston was placed under house arrest. Louis was called to the cardinal's bedside and informed of his favorite's treason. The king sank into a deep depression at the news. One by one, throughout the late summer and early autumn of 1642, the conspirators were brought before the dying Richelieu and interrogated, and one by one they succumbed to the tortuous cross-examination and confessed. Although the cardinal had reams of solid documented evidence, he seemed to take pleasure in extracting confessions from the guilty men. It was a fitting way for him to pass his final months. As for Cinq-Mars, the king's favorite: He went to the scaffold on September 12, 1642.

8

The Torment of His Age

By 1642, Cardinal Richelieu was probably the most hated man in France — and perhaps in all of Europe. The people believed him to be the malign puppet master behind the great death and suffering, the starvation and ravages of war that were now their lot. As if in reflection of the popular perception of him as a monster, Richelieu, in his final weeks, became a grotesque. Because of various ailments, the cardinal had lost so much weight that his appearance had become cadaverous, and he was suffering from "rodent ulcers," a particularly ugly form of skin cancer that attacks the face and hands. Bad circulation had brought on gangrene of the extremities, and he was also tormented by hemorrhoids, to the point that he had the holy relics of the Irish Saint Fiacre, which supposedly had curative powers, brought to him from their resting place in the Cathedral of Meaux. The relics failed to bring the cardinal any relief.

The regime of Cardinal Richelieu ended on December 4, 1642. By the time of his death he had accomplished his lifelong goal to make France the most powerful and respected nation in Europe. Louis XIII, Richelieu's counterpart in forging a new future for France, could not survive without his cardinal's support; he died soon after Richelieu's passing.

Despite his rotting body, the cardinal's mind continued to burn with its characteristic lucidity. He coordinated the war effort from his bed. Occasionally, he was toted to the front in an extravagant litter, which would be placed at an advantageous viewing position atop a hill, where he could preside over the combat. His appearance most likely sent chills through the soldiers of both armies; Richelieu was now little more than a living skeleton swathed in his bright red cardinal's robes, and he bore more than a passing resemblance to the ghastly, hooded and robed, sickle-wielding figure of Death that had become popular in the plague- and violence-ridden Middle Ages.

Death finally came for the cardinal himself on December 4, 1642, while King Louis XIII sat at his bedside in the Palais Cardinal spoon-feeding him egg yolks. Among his final words to the king were these: "Sire, this is my last farewell; in taking leave of Your Majesty I draw comfort from the fact that the kingdom has reached a peak of glory and renown such as it has never known before; your enemies have all been dispersed and humbled." Asked if he would pardon his own enemies, the cardinal replied, "I have none except those of the state." Following these words he vomited a large amount of blood and his doctor was called. "How long?" the cardinal asked. "Within twenty-four hours," the doctor replied, "you will either be cured or be dead." "Well spoken," the cardinal said. It was ten o'clock in the morning; he was dead by noon. (Louis, never far from the cardinal in life, followed him faithfully to the grave five months later.)

Throughout France and Europe there was widespread relief, and a certain superstitious dread and disbelief, at the news of Richelieu's passing; many attributed occult powers to the cardinal and believed that his death was a ruse to fool his enemies and that in truth he might live on, vampirelike, for centuries. Richelieu was indeed dead, however, and after lying in state for a noisome nine days, he was interred in the Church of the Sorbonne. In England, a pamphlet announcing the cardinal's demise called him the "torment of his age."

Richelieu's state, as depicted by many historians, was the state of the future: centralized, compact, and firmly grounded on the principle of national identity.

—J. H. ELLIOTT
historian

Father Joseph, Richelieu's loyal collaborator, had passed away four years previously; perhaps, as he had done so often in life, the Capuchin had gone ahead to smooth the way politically for the cardinal in the afterlife — to ferret out assassins, enlist allies, and confuse the cardinal's enemies. Moments before he died, Father Joseph was heard to mutter the words "Render an account" as if he were anticipating a final judgment. As one of the principal agents of the cardinal's policies, Father Joseph would have had to render an account for Richelieu's actions in order to defend his own. What would the Capuchin have said in praise—or defense—of the cardinal?

The child king Louis XIV (1638—1715), on the hunt with hounds and falcons. The principles of absolutism established by Richelieu were fully realized during his reign.

Cardinal Richelieu, patron of the arts and sciences, and founder of the French Academy, receives scholars outside the Sorbonne, now part of the University of Paris.

Domestically, the cardinal had done more for the French monarchy than the monarchy itself had ever managed to do. By the time of the cardinal's death, the theory of absolutism had become practice. Louis XIV, after the death of his father, inherited a France in which the authority of the king was indeed absolute, having been made so, by Richelieu, at the expense of all the other political entities and representative bodies. According to Richelieu's theory, a stronger king meant a stronger, more unified France, and in certain areas — especially as far as France's national identity was concerned — this was true.

Concerning France's political and military position in the international community, the accomplishments of the cardinal were great and far-reaching. Before the cardinal's ascension to power, France was a despised and bullied weakling, crippled from within by dissension and threatened from without by powerful neighbors. By the time of his death, France was well on its way to replacing Spain

as the dominant nation in Europe. France's preeminence in European affairs was certified by the treaty that ended the Thirty Years' War, the Peace of Westphalia, signed with the Holy Roman Emperor in 1648; and the Peace of the Pyrenees, signed with Spain in 1660 — two treaties the cardinal would have gloated over had he been around to see them.

In rendering his account, Father Joseph would have also pointed out Richelieu's contributions to French culture. The cardinal was a dedicated patron of the arts and sciences throughout his life, and he succeeded in fostering in France an atmosphere in which they flourished. Painting, architecture, drama, poetry, science, and many other artistic and intellectual pursuits and disciplines flowered during Richelieu's regime, and when he died, the city of Paris was well on its way to becoming the center of art and learning in the Western world. Undoubtedly, then, Father Joseph might have argued, France as a nation benefited immensely from the vision and guidance of Richelieu. And his influence

Cardinal Richelieu once said that "great men are more often dangerous than useful in the handling of affairs." Richelieu himself was both.

on France did not die with the cardinal; rather, it remained the dominant political force in that country well into the 18th century.

But what of the French? a devil's advocate might have inquired of the Capuchin during cross-examination. Certainly, as a state, and especially in relation to its European neighbors, France was improved by the cardinal. But as for the French themselves, for the great mass of people who were not of the nobility or the clergy, the cardinal's rule was a heavy burden, and under it the plight of the peasant was not only unrelieved, it was worsened. For the Bourbons, Richelieu was a guardian angel, but for the rest of the people, he was a being of a different nature entirely. The proliferation of popular revolts and uprisings that occurred during the cardinal's final years are the most telling evidence of the effects of his rule on the common population — and a foreshadowing of things to come. Great art and architecture thrived in Paris, to be sure, but the starving peasantry could hardly eat paintings or cathedrals.

Richelieu's absolutist policies only compounded the problem by depriving the Third Estate of political leverage, which instead went to the monarchy. Within France, the ultimate wages of the cardinal's rule were to come more than a century after his death, when the monarchy he had done so much to strengthen — at the expense of the populace — was finally brought down in bloody revolution.

There are also the issues of Cardinal Richelieu's political malice and a cynicism and hypocrisy so ingrained that the cardinal himself was unaware of their existence. His use of the church for political and financial gain was unconscionable. His private residence in Paris, the magnificent Palais Cardinal (the site of the present Palais Royal), was more opulent than any of the king's palaces or mansions, and it stood as a massive and undeniable symbol of the riches of the cardinal — and of his indifference to the impoverished masses of France. He was one of the wealthiest men in Europe when he died, and to the average French citizen, this simply underscored the causes of the Reformation and further debased the reputation of Roman Catholicism. As a representative of Christianity, his ruthlessness is somewhat overshadowed by the atrocities of the Inquisition, but he was certainly one of the deadliest priests in history.

Finally, as a legacy to political science, the cardinal left Europe with the hateful philosophy embodied in the phrase *raison d'état* — in the interests of the state, anything goes. "In judging crimes against the state," the cardinal himself wrote, "it is essential to banish pity." His liberal use of the Bastille and the chopping block was answered a century later by the whistling guillotines of the Terror, and in light of the state-sponsored horrors of 20th-century Europe, raison d'état is a chilling legacy indeed. Perhaps the most apt summation of the career of Cardinal Richelieu was made by Pope Urban VIII, who, upon hearing of the death of the Red Eminence, commented, "If there is a God, Cardinal Richelieu will have much to answer for. If not, he has done very well."

> *Even if conscience can tolerate a notable crime going unpunished, reason of state cannot permit it.*
> —RICHELIEU

Further Reading

Ashley, Maurice. *Louis XIV and the Greatness of France.* London: English Universities Press, 1946.

Auchincloss, Louis. *Richelieu.* New York: Viking Press, 1974.

Bergin, Joseph. *Cardinal Richelieu: Power and the Pursuit of Wealth.* New Haven: Yale University Press, 1985.

Briggs, Robin. *Early Modern France.* New York: Oxford University Press, 1977.

Burckhardt, Carl J. *Richelieu and His Age.* New York: Harcourt Brace Jovanovich, 1970.

Church, William F. *Richelieu and Reason of State.* Princeton, NJ: Princeton University Press, 1972.

Durant, Will, and Ariel Durant. *The Age of Reason Begins.* New York: Simon & Schuster, 1961.

Elliott, J. H. *Richelieu and Olivares.* New York: Cambridge University Press, 1984.

Erlanger, Phillipe. *Richelieu: The Thrust for Power.* New York: Stein & Day, 1968.

Guerard, Albert. *France in the Classical Age.* New York: Harper & Row, 1928.

Huxley, Aldous. *Grey Eminence.* New York: Carroll & Graf, 1985.

Marvick, Elizabeth Wirth. *The Young Richelieu.* Chicago: University of Chicago Press, 1983.

Wedgwood, C. V. *Richelieu and the French Monarchy.* New York: Macmillan, 1962.

Chronology

Sept. 9, 1585	Armand-Jean du Plessis de Richelieu born at the Paris parish of St. Eustache
1597	Enters Collège du Navarre, then Pluvinel's military academy
1602	Named bishop of Luçon in place of his brother
1608	Assumes Luçon bishopric
1610	Henri IV is murdered; Marie de Médicis appointed regent
1615	Richelieu speaks for the Estates General in Paris
1617	Louis XIII assumes throne
1618	Thirty Years' War begins in Bohemia
1624	Richelieu joins royal council
Aug. 1624	Named head of royal council
1627–28	Siege of La Rochelle
Nov. 30, 1630	Day of Dupes
1631	Battle of Castelnaudary; Gaston's forces crushed
1632	Battle of Lützen; Gustavus Adolphus killed
1634	Battle of Nördlingen
May 21, 1635	France declares war on Spain
1636	Imperial forces invade France; Corbie falls; Paris threatened
1638	Naval battle off Lérins Islands; siege of Breisach
1642	Cinq-Mars conspiracy uncovered
Dec. 4, 1642	Cardinal Richelieu dies

Index

Pat Glossop holds an M.A. in comparative literature from the City University of New York. She has lived in London, Paris, Stockholm, and New York, where she is currently on the staff of *Newsweek* magazine. Her articles on broadcasting, travel, and the arts have appeared in numerous publications, including the *Christian Science Monitor,* the *New York Times,* and the *Dallas Time-Herald.*

Arthur M. Schlesinger, jr., taught history at Harvard for many years and is currently Albert Schweitzer Professor of the Humanities at City University of New York. He is the author of numerous highly praised works in American history and has twice been awarded the Pulitzer Prize. He served in the White House as special assistant to Presidents Kennedy and Johnson.